The Companion to the PBS® Television Program

NIAGARA FALLS

AN INTIMATE PORTRAIT

JOHN GRANT *and* RAY JONES

INSIDERS' GUIDE®

GUILFORD, CONNECTICUT
AN IMPRINT OF THE GLOBE PEQUOT PRESS

INSIDERS' GUIDE®

Copyright © 2006 by Western New York Public Broadcasting Association

Text design by Casey Shain

Photo credits: AP/Wide World Photos: 32 (top). Art & Architecture Collection, Miriam and Ira D. Wallach Division of Art, Prints and Photographs, The New York Public Library, Astor, Lenox and Tilden Foundations: 67 (top). © Steven and Joan Blank: 107 (bottom left), 116, 121. Courtesy of Paula Brisco: 107 (center plate). Courtesy of Michelle Brown: 107 (album; bottom middle). Buffalo and Erie County Historical Society: 80 (bottom), 88. Corcoran Gallery of Art, Washington, D.C.: 70–71. Courtesy of DeWitt Clinton High School, © 1905 C. Y. Turner: 36 (top). © Digital Attractions, Inc.: 123. Courtesy of Lisa and Murray Egan: 107 (top right). © Eileen Koteras Elibol: 42, 68, 73 (back), 78, 97. Photographs by Eileen Koteras Elibol © WNED-TV: i, iii–vi, 6, 7 (back), 9, 11 (bottom), 13, 15–16, 18, 20, 27 (bottom), 29, 31, 32 (back), 34, 37, 38–39 (back), 41 (back), 48–49 (back), 52 (back), 55 (back), 58, 59 (back), 60 (barrel), 65, 75, 77, 83, 86 (back), 89, 93, 94–95 (back), 99, 100 (back), 101–2, 104–5, 108, 112–14, 118–19, 125–27, 130, 132, 134–35, 137, 138–42, 144–52, 54. Courtesy of Kathy Gousios Haugh: 107 (top middle). Library and Archives Canada/Credit: Théophile Hamel/C-014305: 25 (bottom). Library of Congress, LC-USZ62-90556: 27 (top). LOC, LC-USZ62-118438: 32 (top). LOC, LC-USZ62-127674: 32 (bottom). LOC, LC-USZ62-36895: 73 (top). LOC, LC-amrvg vg60 (0007-0016): 74. LOC, LC-USZ62-98128: 84 (top). LOC, DIG-ggbain-04851: 84 (bottom). LOC, LC-USZC4-12227: 111 (bottom). © Stanford Lipsey: 8. Courtesy of Map Collection, Yale University Library: 24. Courtesy of Niagara Falls (Ontario) Public Library: 4–5, 7 (inset), 10, 14, 17, 21–22, 26, 30, 33, 36 (bottom), 39 (inset), 40, 44, 46–47, 48 (inset), 49 (inset), 50, 52 (right), 53–54, 55 (bottom), 56–57, 59, 60 (1901 photo), 61–63, 64 (bottom), 80–81 (top), 85, 87, 90, 94 (inset), 98, 109, 122, 124, 129, 131, 143. Courtesy of Niagara Falls (Ontario) Public Library, Consent given to NFPL by George Bailey: 110, 111 (top). Courtesy of the N.Y. Power Authority: 100. Courtesy of Norma Seal: 107 (center left, center right, bottom right). Courtesy of the Theodore Roosevelt Inaugural Site Foundation–Buffalo, N.Y.: 66, 67 (back, bottom). Courtesy of Lynn and Jeff Zelem: 107 (top left).

Video captures: © WNED-TV: 2, 11 (top), 25 (top), 41, 64 (top), 92, 95, 115, 117.

Library of Congress Cataloging-in-Publication Data
Grant, John, 1948–
    Niagara falls: an intimate portrait/John Grant and Ray Jones.—1st ed.
        p. cm.
    "The Companion to the PBS Television Program."
    Includes index.
    ISBN 0-7627-4025-6
    1. Niagara Falls (N.Y. and Ont.)—History. 2. Niagara Falls (N.Y. and Ont.)—Pictorial works.
I. Jones, Ray, 1948– . II. Title.
F127.N8G69 2006
971.3'39—dc22
                                                                    2005032616

Manufactured in China
First Edition/First Printing

Contents

Foreword

Welcome to *Niagara Falls: An Intimate Portrait*, the companion to the exciting WNED/PBS television special on one of the world's greatest and best-known wonders. As you turn these pages, you'll experience Niagara Falls as a natural phenomenon of immense power and as a cultural force of great historic importance. Consisting of two mighty cataracts—the American and Canadian, or Horseshoe—Niagara Falls has stunned countless visitors, but it is far more than a nearly mile-wide stretch of breathtaking scenery and a magnet for international tourism. It is a widely recognized icon for the New World, a unifying bridge between the United States and Canada, and an enduring symbol of environmental stewardship.

Niagara Falls forms the heart of a binational community that cannot fail to impress with its warm hospitality, lively cultural offerings, fascinating architecture, and, of course, extraordinary natural beauty. The impact of the falls on generations of adventurers, scientists, artists, tourists, and local peoples has shaped this vibrant region as we know it today. *Niagara Falls: An Intimate Portrait* tells how water draining from the continental interior in unimaginable quantities has sculpted not just the rocks of a grand waterfall and a breathtaking gorge but an entire way of life.

In *Niagara Falls: An Intimate Portrait* you'll meet Father Louis Hennepin, the seventeenth-century monk said by some to have been the first European to lay eyes on the great falls; John Roebling, whose "wire rope" made it possible to span the Niagara Gorge with a suspension bridge; and Nikola Tesla, whose alternating-current generators turned the falls into North America's most potent electric power source. You'll walk across the yawning gorge on

a wire with the daredevil nineteenth-century acrobat Charles Blondin and plunge over the brink of the falls with Annie Taylor, the retirement-age teacher who was the first to—unwisely we now believe—challenge Niagara in a wooden barrel. Of course, everyone who comes to Niagara Falls—whether to paint a masterpiece like Frederic Edwin Church, make a movie like Marilyn Monroe, or enjoy a honeymoon like many, many others—has stories of their own, and you'll hear some of those as well.

As the public broadcaster serving western New York and southern Ontario, WNED is proud to celebrate—both on PBS and in this book—the awe-inspiring wonder of Niagara Falls and the people it has influenced. This celebration would not have been possible without the dedication and hard work of many individuals. Our special thanks and acknowledgment to John Grant, Larry Hott, Diane Garey, and Ken Chowder for an outstanding job on the *Niagara Falls* television production and to John Grant, Ray Jones, and photographer Eileen Koteras Elibol for masterfully capturing the magnificence of the falls in the companion text *Niagara Falls: An Intimate Portrait*. Appreciation is also extended to the Niagara Parks Commission, Niagara Tourism and Convention Corporation, Ciminelli Real Estate Corporation, and PBS for investments that made these projects reality. And special thanks to New York State Senator George D. Maziarz and Jim Williams, chairman of the Niagara Parks Commission, for their support for this project.

As those who reside here already know, Niagara Falls is a grand treasure that enriches our lives in countless ways. We're happy to share—via the airwaves and the printed page—that gift with you. Enjoy.

Donald K. Boswell
President and CEO, WNED-TV

Marriage
of the
Waters

Symbol of a Continent

**There's so much to tell because everything ties together.
It's about the earth. It's about nature. It's about people.**

—*Jolene Rickard, Tuscarora Tribe*

Each of Earth's continents has at least one natural feature that stands out in our minds as a symbol for all its diverse lands and peoples. For Africa, that feature is probably the Nile; for Asia, Mount Everest; for Australia, Uluru (Ayers Rock); for South America, the Amazon; for Europe, the Alps or, perhaps, the Greek Isles. Here in North America, however, the choice may at first seem a little more difficult. Depending on where you live and how much of this great continent you've seen, you may at first favor the Mississippi River, the Canadian Rockies, or maybe Alaska's Mount McKinley. But if you give the question much consideration at all, the choices can easily be reduced to one.

A few miles from the city of Buffalo, New York, and just across Lake Ontario from Toronto is a natural phenomenon so majestic and powerful that every year it strikes millions of people speechless with awe. Tourists flock from every state in the Union, every Canadian province, and literally every nation on earth just to see and experience it. Children the world over have heard of this place and, no doubt, have dreamed of traveling to Ontario or New York to stand before it and feel its spray touch their faces. The phenomenon in question is, of course, Niagara Falls.

Actually a pair of falls, the American and Horseshoe (also known as the Canadian Falls), one on either side of the border between the United States and Canada, they form what is arguably the world's most famous and popular natural wonder. And why shouldn't it be? Fed by the overflow from four of the Earth's

Throbbing heart of a great continent, Niagara Falls pumps 750,000 gallons of water per second toward the Atlantic.

mightiest lakes, the falls are impressive indeed. More than forty million gallons of water plunge over them every minute, dropping more than 180 feet in a mighty white curtain. Every minute as much as 180,000 tons of water hit the rocks and the surface of the Niagara River below, throwing up a towering plume of mist and a thunderous roar that can be heard for miles. This unforgettable display of nature's raw power has inspired poets, scientists, conservationists, politicians, and countless ordinary citizens—not to mention generations of young couples who have flocked to the falls to get married and honeymoon.

Niagara Falls seems to generate a cultural magnetism that pulls people to it and then forever links them to this extraordinary place, to one another, and to their destinies. Friar Louis Hennepin, a companion of the intrepid explorer La Salle, came here in 1678 and later earned a living by entertaining credulous Europeans with fanciful descriptions of the falls. The warriors of France, England, Canada, the United States, and several Native American nations came here, too, and fought many bloody battles over Niagara Falls and the strategic portage that circumvented it. In 1860 Britain's Prince of Wales came to enjoy the spectacle. Later in the nineteenth century, Nikola Tesla, a prince of the electrical sciences, came to Niagara and staked his reputation on an alternating-current hydroelectric plant at the foot of the falls. President William McKinley paid the falls a visit in 1901 shortly before he was shot by an assassin at the Pan-American Exposition in Buffalo. Marilyn Monroe took a walk beside the falls in 1952 and set a new standard for sensuality.

The falls have also attracted many daredevils. In 1859 the Great Blondin, the famed French tightrope artist, defied clouds of mist, tricky winds, and gravity itself to walk over the yawning gulf carved out by the falls. His likewise famous competitor, Farini, joined him the following year in a remarkable display of one-upmanship that had them carrying stoves out over the Niagara Gorge to cook their dinners and washing machines to do their laundry. Surprisingly, Blondin and Farini each lived to a ripe old age—unlike many of the brave fools who have challenged the falls in pickle barrels, oil drums, and kayaks and even on Jet Skis. One who did survive was Annie Edson Taylor, a sixty-two-year-old woman who spilled over the falls in an oak cask in 1901. She was the first to attempt such a stunt but, unfortunately, not the last.

Of course, the daredevils most commonly seen at Niagara Falls are the legions of honeymooners who, having taken the plunge, so to speak, are testing the waters of matrimony. Napoleon's younger brother Jerome and his wife are said to have honeymooned here in 1803. They may or may not have been the first newlyweds to have their blood stirred by the thrill of Niagara Falls, but they certainly would not be the last. It is said that more than 50,000 couples honeymoon here each year. Given the earthy, eminently physical power of the falls, it is not hard to understand why.

Above the Plume

Niagara Falls is full of energy, and there's a charge you get when you come here. Everyone gets it. It's a lure, a magnet, and you're drawn to it. Your passions are raised, and yet somehow you're sorry.

—Bill Irwin, historian

The Great Lakes are one of the profound earthly details that can be easily identified from the International Space Station in orbit far above the planet. Sharp-eyed astronauts may be able to make out the 30-mile-wide neck of land that separates the two fish-shaped eastern lakes, but it is unlikely they will see the river that cuts across this narrow feature. Passengers on airliners flying east or west between Boston and Detroit or Montreal and Chicago may spot this streak of blue, and any who are in the least familiar with the geography of the United States and Canada will know that this short but extraordinary water channel is the Niagara River, which links Lakes Erie and Ontario. Those who recognize the river are likely to crane their necks and press their faces against the glass, searching for a white plume rising from the water's surface. Find the plume, and they can be sure they are looking down on Niagara Falls.

Seeing the falls from the air is a thrill, and it is educational in a number of important ways. That is why so many Niagara Falls visitors opt to enjoy North America's most famous natural wonder from above. More than a few choose to see it through the windows of a helicopter. Ruedi Hafen has been offering helicopter rides over the Niagara River, Gorge, and Falls since 1981. His company, Niagara Helicopters, serves about 100,000 passengers a year.

"I do a lot of the flying myself," says Hafen. "I never get tired of flying over the falls and sharing that experience with people."

Located in Canada several miles from the falls but within easy reach of all the tourist hotels, Niagara Helicopters is a beehive of activity nearly every day. Painted in a rainbow of colors, the helicopters take to the air vertically, like dragonflies, then sweep westward toward the Niagara River.

"The first thing we do is find the river," says Hafen. "Then we let it show us the way to the falls."

As the helicopter quickly gains altitude, it is possible to see Lake Ontario to the north and on the south a hint of Lake Erie. The land between the lakes is obviously no wilderness. It shows the imprint of nearly three centuries of heavy human use and development. There are streets and highways cutting across from the east, west, north, and south, each of them crawling with antlike processions of cars and trucks. There are houses and hotels, restaurants and shopping centers, public buildings and factories; and slicing through, as if ignoring it all, is the Niagara River. In the south the river forms a sparkling aqua ribbon and in the north a tossing white jumble of rapids rushing through a deep gorge. The helicopter intersects the river about halfway along the gorge and then turns toward a place where that water appears to be boiling. Actually, what looks like steam is really mist, and the mass of roiling water throwing it skyward is Niagara Falls.

"On the right-hand side is a beautiful view of the Niagara Whirlpool," says Hafen, pointing toward a swirl of blue that suggests an enormous storm drain. "And over there is our huge power complex, the largest in North America. This view gives you a good idea of how it all works. The international control dam feeds water from the river into underground tunnels about 45 feet in diameter. These carry it under the city of Niagara Falls, New York, and down to the power stations."

There's plenty more. "You can also see the Whirlpool Golf Course, the cable car, our beautiful hotels, casinos, and the other great Niagara attractions," says Hafen, who's obviously proud of the community. "Niagara Falls is open all year for tourism."

All this is very interesting, but passengers might be forgiven if, in their excitement

Aerial views of the falls were once available only as art or souvenirs like the vintage postcards above and the antique panorama below.

Veteran helicopter pilot Ruedi Hafen (lower right) enjoys treating his passengers to the view of a lifetime— Niagara Falls from the air.

and anticipation, they miss some of the narrative. The reason for taking the flight—the star of the show—is just up ahead, just beyond the graceful arch of the Rainbow Bridge.

"This is the view of all views in the world," says Hafen. "We're just flying by the American Falls and Goat Island. Then there's Canadian Falls, also called Horseshoe Falls. From up here it's easy to see why they call it Horseshoe Falls. It really has the shape of a horseshoe."

Some in the helicopter may have taken note of the shape, but if so, they don't acknowledge it. They are too busy looking.

"Most of the time people don't say very much because they're so taken with the view, by the emotion of it. The feeling is just too much for them."

Hafen is right about the passengers not commenting on the view. After all, what is there for them to say? It is indescribable.

Linchpin of the Great Lakes

As a natural phenomenon, Niagara Falls is closely linked to the Great Lakes. The Niagara River, which flows over the falls, is not a river at all in the strictest sense of the word. Rather it is a strait connecting two of the lakes—Erie and Ontario. Water flows from the upper four lakes (Superior, Michigan, Huron, and Erie) over the falls into Lake Ontario and from there down the St. Lawrence River to the Atlantic Ocean.

Covering 95,000 square miles of the continental heartland in a cold, blue blanket, the Great Lakes comprise the largest open expanse of inland water on the planet. Created by glaciers over a period of 100,000 years or more, they impound approximately 20 percent—some 5,500 cubic miles, or 6,000 trillion gallons—of the Earth's fresh water.

Only about 1 percent of the lakes' water flows down through the Niagara and St. Lawrence Rivers each

Romantic-era depiction of Niagara Gorge.

year. The lake levels remain relatively constant, but since relatively few rivers flow into them, the lakes are replenished largely by groundwater seeping in from surrounding lands.

The elevations of the lakes vary. Superior is about 23 feet higher than Michigan and Huron, which are actually one big lake connected by the 5-mile-wide Straits of Mackinac. The water level drops another 8 feet at Erie, then 326 additional feet before it reaches Lake Ontario. More than half the total elevation loss of about 359 feet from Lake Superior to Lake Ontario takes place quite suddenly at Niagara Falls, where the water drops 180 feet. In this way, the falls play an integral role in the drainage of the North American interior.

Maid of the Mist

Tourists, tourists, tourists. People come here from every part of the world, and sometimes you wonder if there are that many people on the whole planet.

—Richard Schuyler, captain, Maid of the Mist

Increasing numbers of tourists are electing to see Niagara Falls from the air, but many still prefer to view this world-renowned spectacle from another, very different perspective—the water. Approaching Niagara's torrential cliffs on a boat is invariably a damp and wave-tossed experience, but people have been doing it for more than 150 years. Today, just as they did in the mid-nineteenth century, visitors ride into the maw of the great Horseshoe Falls aboard a vessel called *Maid of the Mist*. Perhaps the longest-playing thrill ride on the continent, the *Maid* is in fact a whole fleet of small excursion craft, all with the same name.

There have been many earlier *Maids*. Launched in 1846, the original *Maid of the Mist* was meant to serve as a

Its decks crowded with sightseers, the Maid of the Mist *(opposite) approaches the tumbled boulders of American Falls (below).*

ferry. It had carried passengers back and forth across the Niagara River for only a couple of years, however, before completion of a bridge put the ferry service out of business. The *Maid*'s hard-pressed owners then turned the vessel into an excursion boat and began to offer tours of Niagara Falls.

The concept proved so successful that a second *Maid* was launched in 1854, and it had a significant advantage over its predecessor—steam. A paddle wheeler with a single boiler and smokestack, the *Maid of the Mist II* had the power to keep just beyond reach of the most turbulent waters. This meant she could go much closer to Horseshoe Falls and provide her passengers with an even more astonishing view.

The captains of today's *Maids*, who can rely on muscular diesel engines, shake their heads at the thought of piloting a steamboat into the basin of the Horseshoe. They know only too well that it takes a vessel with considerable power to navigate the swirling currents below the falls. It also takes great skill.

"The current is pretty strong," says John Williams, a veteran mariner with many years of experience on the Great Lakes and the Niagara River. Williams has been a *Maid of the Mist* captain for about fifteen years. "No matter where you've worked before, nothing can really prepare you for taking a boat though a big waterfall. It takes skill and practice, but it's not too difficult as long as you stay in the middle and keep out of the back eddies."

Even with all his years on the water, Williams would not try to accomplish the feat that an earlier *Maid* captain named Joel Robinson attempted in 1861—taking a large boat downstream through the Niagara Gorge and its killer Whirlpool Rapids.

The steam-powered *Maid of the Mist II* operated profitably for several years, but when the Civil War broke out and the tourist trade dried up, she was sold to a Canadian firm. To complete the deal, the 72-foot steamer had to be delivered to Lake Ontario, and the only way to get her there was a perilous—in fact, seemingly impossible—run through the Niagara Gorge. Robinson had only recently seen the great acrobat Blondin do what appeared to be impossible by walking across the gorge on a rope. Robinson himself had already earned a reputation for derring-do by rowing a small skiff to the very brink of the Horseshoe to prevent a stranded boater from being swept over the falls to an almost certain death. Now he agreed, with the help of two volunteer crewmen, to take the helm of the *Maid* and challenge the gorge.

At three o'clock in the afternoon on June 15, 1861, Robinson gave the order to cast off into the rapids, and almost immediately lost control of his little ship. Even under a full head of steam, the *Maid*'s paddle wheel made no impression whatever on the river, and the vessel was tossed around in the rapids like a child's toy. At one point she heeled over on her side and an enormous wave swept over her, carrying away her stack. Meanwhile, Robinson and his companions rolled around inside the boat like marbles in a cigar box. Finally—and quite miraculously—the *Maid* popped out of the whirlpool and into the chute of the lower rapids. A small bird caught in a great wind, she blew down through the remainder of the gorge, reaching the relatively placid waters of Lake Ontario in only a few minutes.

Following his wild race through the gorge, Robinson could barely speak for weeks. Even after he recovered his voice, he was a completely changed man. Previously ebullient and gregarious, he became introspective and private. Robinson had confronted something in the Niagara Gorge that he would never find words to adequately describe. The Greek gods of old warned mariners not to look upon the face of the Gorgon, but Robinson had seen it. Once known as the most courageous man on the river, he never again dipped his toe in the Niagara.

The *Maid of the Mist* excursions started up again in 1885, and since then thousands of tourists have descended into the Niagara Gorge to experience its wonders—and terrors—for themselves. Wisely, they travel upriver toward the falls rather than downriver toward the lake as Robinson did, but what they see along the way can be life changing. Just as no previous maritime experience can fully prepare a captain to navigate the Horseshoe, nothing at all can prepare a person for an in-the-face view of Niagara Falls.

Maid of the Mist *captains Richard Schuyler (left) and John Williams regularly steer passengers through rainbowed torrents to the foot of the falls, but they would never attempt a wild run down through the gorge like that of an earlier Maid in 1861 (opposite).*

Employing the skills and confidence they have gained through years of challenging the tricky Niagara currents, the *Maid* captains can hold their vessels in the swirling cauldron of the Horseshoe for several minutes at a time. Typically they approach within a few hundred feet of the falls, but they dare not test fate by going any closer. Even so, *Maid* passengers may think that all the waters of the upper Great Lakes are tumbling down on top of them.

"We're probably at least a hundred yards from the corner of the falls at any one time, so we have quite a margin of safety here," says Williams. "It's a bit of an optical illusion how close we get. We're a lot farther back than it looks, but in all this spray, people don't know the difference. It's quite a show for them."

Passengers expect to get a little wet. That is a predictable and, for most, enjoyable part of the trip. To keep them from getting not just damp but laundry-wringer drenched, passengers are protected in part by plastic ponchos handed out as they get onboard the *Maid*. The ponchos are blue and make an attractive match for the broad blue stripe running down the side of the boat and for the Niagara River's vivid blue water.

"They weren't always blue," says Williams. "Back in the 1970s we handed out heavy dark raincoats, but with all this spray, they developed an odor. So we tried other types of cloaks and materials. Finally we decided to go with the blue ponchos and just throw them away afterward. A lot of people keep them and take them home as souvenirs. You can go to Disney World or a parade thousands of miles from here and see someone wearing a *Maid of the Mist* raincoat."

Of course, passengers take from their Niagara experiences something far more valuable than a plastic raincoat—memories that don't grow moldy with time. Launched during the 1990s, the all-steel *Maid of the Mist VI* and *VII* can carry more than 500 passengers each, and it is likely safe to say that every passenger responds to the falls in his or her own unique way. You can see it in their faces. Some wear the slack-jawed expressions of awestruck children. Others appear to be studying the falls as if it were a Monet hanging in a gallery. Still others seem unable to gaze at the immense phenomenon for more than a few moments at a stretch. Then they must look away. Have they, like Robinson, been struck by some indescribable terror? Or have they merely turned aside to wipe the spray from their eyes?

Thunderbeings

The falls represent a force of nature that can't be tamed.

—*Jolene Rickard, Tuscarora Tribe*

Native Americans have always held deep reverence for Niagara Falls. They lived on the banks of the falls for centuries, and to them it was the home of the Thunderbeings. Unlike the Gorgons of Greek myth, the Thunderbeings were creators rather than destroyers. Wielding great bolts of lightning, they killed an evil Giant Horned Serpent, and the arc of his fallen body formed Horseshoe Falls.

A different story concerning the creation of the falls was once told, though almost certainly not by Native Americans. According to this legend, a people living near the falls began to die from a mysterious ailment, and they appealed to their Thunder God for help. To catch the god's attention, they sent fruit and wild game over the falls in canoes. When this failed to halt the spread of the disease, they sent a beautiful maiden named Lelawalo over the falls. Lelawalo fell into the arms of the god's amorous son, who extracted a promise from her to marry him. In return he revealed the slithery source of her tribe's problems: A giant water serpent was poisoning their drinking water, and anyone who died from the poison would be eaten by the snake. Lelawalo got word of this to her family and friends, and they were able to ambush the snake and mortally wound it with spears. Before it died, the serpent swam to the brink of the falls, where its body settled in the shape of a horseshoe.

Perhaps not surprisingly, Lelawalo is also known as the Maid of the Mist, and it is said this is how the famous excursion boats got their names. Others say the story was fabricated by greedy nineteenth-century Niagara businessmen, who used it to attract gullible tourists. American Indians agree with the latter interpretation and take particular exception to the suggestion that their people ever practiced human sacrifice.

"The Europeans *said* we sacrificed a beautiful Indian woman by sending her over the falls," says Eli Rickard of the Tuscarora, a Niagara tribe with a reservation near the falls. "They called her spirit the Maid of the Mist. Well, like most Indian men, I like Indian women— no way would I ever send one over the falls. *Our* story

According to Native American myth, sacred beings formed the curve of the great Horseshoe from the body of a giant serpent. Whatever legends animate their beliefs, Niagara visitors are likely to find spiritual meaning in the power and beauty of the falls.

was about a woman who went over the falls in a canoe but was actually saved by the spirits. They felt compassion for her and gave her life back. To us the falls represent life—the life-giving powers of the universe. But to the white man it represents death—the power of the universe to kill."

Behind the Wall

Those who see the falls from the deck of the *Maid of the Mist* know their immense power can be both inspiring and frightening. So, too, do those who see them from the closest vantage

Cave of the Winds in Winter, Niagara Falls.

point of all—from the Cave of the Winds, which takes visitors behind the great wall of water.

The original Cave of the Winds was a natural overhang of hard dolomite stone that extended a considerable distance behind Bridal Veil Falls on the American side of the Niagara cataract. It was discovered early in the nineteenth century by local adventure seekers who spotted it from Goat Island, climbed down into the Niagara Gorge, and clambered into the cave. Standing behind the great sheet of luminous water filled them with wonder, and its deafening roar caused them to name the place Aeolus' Cave after the Greek god of wind. Soon after, the name was changed to the somewhat friendlier and more easily pronounced Cave of the Winds. By 1879 the owners of Goat Island started charging cave visitors what then seemed an outrageous admission price—$1.00 a head. Even so, few complained that the experience was not worth the money. The attraction remained hugely popular until the very same erosive forces that had created the cave also destroyed it. Increasingly plagued by rockfalls that on more than one occasion injured or killed tourists, the cave was destroyed by a carefully controlled dynamite blast in 1955.

An early-twentieth-century postcard (left) shows the Cave of the Winds draped in winter ice. Restored annually after the spring thaw, an extensive wooden stairway (opposite) now leads visitors behind Bridal Veil and Luna Falls.

The Iroquois Confederacy

One of the oldest participatory democracies in the world, the Iroquois Confederacy is believed to have been founded about the middle of the twelfth century, perhaps 350 years before Columbus set foot in the Americas. Composed of peoples who had settled in what is now upstate New York and southern Canada—the Mohawks, Senecas, Onondagas, Oneidas, Cayugas, and later the Tuscaroras—the confederacy was brought together after decades of destructive warfare among the member nations.

The basis of the confederacy is the *Gayaneshakgowa,* or "Great Law of Peace," a complex oral constitution that sets out the expectations and responsibilities of each nation and explains how they are to live together peacefully. The Great Law established two representative bodies, or brotherhoods, that regulate justice and deal with non-Iroquois nations while respecting the sovereignty of the member nations. The idea was to assemble leaders in forums where "thinking replaces violence."

The *Gayaneshakgowa* also established nine clans: Wolf, Hawk, Bear, Beaver, Deer, Eel, Turtle, Heron, and Snipe, which are common to several though not all the Iroquois Nations. According to the Great Law, members of each clan, regardless of their tribal affiliation, are considered blood kin and cannot marry one another. No one nation has all nine clans. The Senecas have the most, with eight; the Oneidas and Mohawks have the least, just three each. This dual relationship, to both clan and nation, was intended to discourage feuds.

The women of each clan elect men to represent the clan at the Great Council, which meets in a location central to the territory of the confederacy. The Mohawk and Seneca nations meet in one brotherhood—similar to a legislative body—initiating all laws and actions. The Cayugas and Oneidas meet in a separate brotherhood, or caucus, to deliberate. Within each body, if agreement cannot be reached, a "sense of the council" is established. The Onondagas, or "firekeepers," arbitrate the differences between the two bodies. (The French called the Onondagas the "Neutrals" because they cast the deciding vote.)

The success of this system can be seen in its continued use today. American admiration for the confederacy's structure was evident in the respect the Continental Congress showed Iroquois leaders who were invited to Philadelphia in 1776 when the future of an independent United States was being deliberated. Years later, members of the Constitutional Convention carefully studied the confederacy before framing the structure of the U.S. government.

Today's Cave of the Winds is not really a cave at all, but rather a series of wooden staircases, platforms, and walkways that snake behind the Bridal Veil and Luna segments of the American Falls. A tour of this damp labyrinth is the highlight of any outing in New York's Niagara Reservation State Park on Goat Island. However, keeping the cave open and making the tours possible takes a lot of work.

Winter is unfriendly to the cave, and any wooden structures that are not removed before the attraction closes down at the end of the autumn season will be ripped away by ice and washed down the river. To cut down on the loss of wood and materials, everything is pulled apart and stored each fall and then reassembled in spring. Rebuilding the "cave" and repairing the damage done by ice and snow can take up to six weeks. In a typical year, the park may spend more than $15,000 on the wood used to reconstruct the serpentine passageway. Before all the sawing and pounding is complete, workers will have used as many as six fifty-pound boxes of sixteen-penny nails.

Those who visit during warm-weather months may not be aware of how much effort it takes to maintain the cave, but they are invariably happy to have had the opportunity to see it. Seeing the Cave of the Winds is considered a rite of passage for Niagara Falls tourists. After all, where else can you walk right into a waterfall, especially one like this?

For safety's sake, guides lead visitors down the wooden steps and along the walkways, which come as close as 15 feet to the crashing waters. Just as onboard the *Maid of the Mist*, everyone is dressed in rain gear, but it is only marginally helpful. Many get soaked to the skin by the ubiquitous spray, but they may not notice they are wet until later—and perhaps not even then. The experience itself takes precedence over wet clothing and all other considerations. Standing only a few feet from so much natural violence, it is impossible not to think that you are staring into the very face of the Giant Horned Serpent, the Gorgon, or whatever you choose to call it.

The legend of the Indian maiden Lelawalo (above), who sought divine aid for her ailing tribe by riding over the falls in a canoe, was concocted by early nineteenth-century businessmen to draw tourists to moneymaking attractions such as the Cave of the Winds. Visitors paid a dollar each to use the enclosed stairway (below) that provided access to the cave.

In *the* Beginning

Waterfall on a Plain

When you drive here, you'll notice that the geography is flat. This is a floodplain. Most waterfalls are runoff from the mountains and are part of a river tributary, but there are no mountains around here, and the Niagara doesn't have any tributaries. It's kind of mind-boggling when you look at the falls, and you just can't help wondering: Where does all this water come from?

—*John Williams, captain,* Maid of the Mist

In the beginning, Niagara was wilderness. So was the rest of North America, but this particular bit of wilderness was stupendous. Here the waters of four enormous lakes, containing nearly two-thirds of all the fresh water on the entire continent, rush over the rocky bottom of the Niagara River. Beginning at the far northeastern end of Lake Erie and for 20 miles thereafter, it flows over a nearly level grade. Then the bottom drops out, and with breathtaking suddenness the great mass of water dives down some twenty stories, plunging into a roiling pool more than 200 feet deep.

It was not always this way, of course. Niagara Falls is a young geological feature— only about 12,500 years old. Compared with the 500-million-year-old North American continent, which gave birth to it, Niagara is a mere infant, albeit a loud and muscular one. It is the child not just of an incredibly ancient and colossal landmass but also of the rarest of circumstances.

Hundreds of millions of years ago, in the region we now know as New York and Ontario, weathering mountains dumped sediment into shallow lakes and seas, building up layers of soft shale and capping it with a much harder rock called dolomite. These materials eventually formed the extremely massive stony block now

Child of the Ice Age, Niagara's thunderous cataract drains four of the Great Lakes and a large portion of the North American interior.

referred to as the Niagara Escarpment. Dozens of miles wide and hundreds of feet thick, the escarpment serves as a natural dam holding back the waters of the upper Great Lakes. But here we get ahead of our story.

The Great Lakes themselves are quite young. They owe their existence to a profound change in the planetary climate that took place about one million years ago when, for reasons that scientists have still not fully explained, the earth suddenly grew much colder. In northern latitudes the summer sun was no longer warm enough to melt the snow left over from winter, and eventually it accumulated into frozen sheets as much as 2 miles thick. Several times since the big chill set in, the giant ice sheets have advanced across the northern half of the continent, only to retreat when the weather warmed up sufficiently to drive back the ice. The last such glacial advance ended about 15,000 years ago, and when the ice had finally melted, it left behind a greatly altered landscape. In the Midwest the heavy glaciers had bulldozed enormous depressions, some of them hundreds of miles wide. The cold water draining from the dying glaciers then filled the depressions to form Lakes Ontario, Erie, Huron, Michigan, and Superior as well as thousands of smaller lakes.

At first the overflow from the big lakes washed down through what is now Lake Champlain and into the Hudson River. The ragged scars left behind by the flooding this caused can still be seen in the Hudson Valley. As the ice fell back beyond the St. Lawrence River, Lake Ontario abandoned the Hudson and found its rightful outlet. For a while the waters of the upper lakes flowed toward the St. Lawrence and the Atlantic through south-

A DISTANT VIEW OF THE FALLS OF NIAGARA

western Ontario, but eventually they settled into the channel of the Niagara River.

Because the dolomite over which the Niagara River flows was laid down in almost perfectly horizontal layers, it is highly resistant to erosion. This means that most of the erosion takes place when the water drops off the edge of the dolomite and reaches the soft shale underneath. Once lake water started pouring through the 30-mile-long river and falling over the 200-foot-high escarpment into Lake Ontario, the shale began to wash away. This left blocks of dolomite hanging out over the cliff; without the support of the shale, they began to break off and fall into what soon became the Niagara Gorge. Over the millennia, the water has chiseled away at the shale and dolomite at a rate of up to 6 feet a year, creating a gorge 7 miles long.

When the process of carving out the gorge began more than 12,000 years ago, the falls dropped almost directly into Lake Ontario. At that time, humans had migrated to North America only recently. There may have still been herds of wooly mammoths and mastodons roaming the continent, but they would soon be extinct.

By the time the pyramids were built in Egypt, approximately 4,500 years ago, the river had gouged out a gorge several miles long. Then came a cataclysmic event. Retreating in a more or less southwesterly direction, the falls reached a much older riverbed that the

The flat-top cliffs shown in the nineteenth-century illustration above and photograph opposite consist of erosion-prone shale capped by a layer of much harder rock known as dolomite.

305:—AERO CABLE OVER WHIRLPOOL RAPIDS, NIAGARA FALLS.

In operation since 1916, Niagara's famed Spanish Aero Car provides adventurous sightseers with a bird's-eye view of Whirlpool Basin, where the turbulent river makes a ninety-degree turn.

glaciers had buried and filled with gravel, talus, and other easily eroded materials. Probably begun with the thunderous collapse of a thin wall of shale and dolomite, the ensuing washout likely took only a few days—perhaps only a few hours. When it was over and the river had torn away the glacial debris, it left behind the famous Whirlpool Basin, where a swirling vortex of blue-green water marks an abrupt, 90-degree change in the course of the Niagara River. Southeast of the basin are the Whirlpool Rapids, one of the world's best-known and most dangerous stretches of white water. The rapids were likely excavated in the same geological upheaval that created the basin.

When the Roman Empire was founded about 2,000 years ago, the Niagara River was hacking away at the rocks just north of the existing Rainbow Bridge and a couple of miles north of the current position of the falls. Roughly 500 years ago the rapidly retreating brink encountered an outcropping of harder, less easily eroded stone. This obstacle, known today as Goat Island, caused the river channel to split and created American Falls on the east side of the river and Horseshoe Falls on the west.

Currently, the brink of the American Falls is 176 feet high and 1,060 feet across; Horseshoe Falls is 185 feet high and 2,200 feet—almost half a mile—across. The volume of water dropping over Horseshoe Falls is roughly 180,000 cubic feet per second when the flow of the Niagara River peaks. That is about nine times the volume tumbling over the American Falls—about 20,000 cubic feet per second at peak flow. As a result, Horseshoe Falls erodes faster than the American Falls. During the nineteenth century the brink of Horseshoe Falls was thought to be retreating at an average rate of more than 5 feet each year. Now that 50 percent of the Niagara's volume has been diverted into tunnels for use in hydroelectric plants, however, the brink is retreating at a much slower rate, perhaps only about 1 foot per year.

The future of Niagara Falls is unclear. The only thing certain is that dramatic changes will occur. Horseshoe Falls will continue to recede, while a shifting riverbed will eventually dry up American Falls. It may take Horseshoe Falls another 15,000 years to move back another 4 miles, but at that point it will have cut through all the erosion-resistant limestone underlying the Niagara Escarpment. The softer rocks behind the escarpment will offer less resistance to the fast-flowing river, which could wash it away in a relatively short period. Instead of dropping over a falls, the waters of Lake Erie will roll and toss toward Lake Ontario over a series of rapids. In time, global climate change and drier weather in the Midwest may reduce the volume and expanse of all the Great Lakes until little is left but a river valley, of which the Niagara will be one small part.

Rumors of a Terrible Majesty

Early visitors to the falls had difficulty telling others what they had seen. They had no language, no words to describe it, so they fell back on a description of their feelings. They spoke of being confused, overwhelmed, or overpowered.

—Elizabeth McKinsey, author

In 1534, little more than a generation after Columbus discovered America, a bold Frenchman named Jacques Cartier set out across the Atlantic to see the New World for himself. Exploring the lower reaches of what is now known as the St. Lawrence River, Cartier befriended Native Americans he met along the shore and questioned them about the interior of the giant landmass that stood before him. They described a country overflowing with gold, silver, copper, and spices. Though Cartier may have been anxious to believe them, these claims would, in the course of time, prove to have been largely untrue. But Cartier likely heard other stories as well—of mighty plains of fresh water so broad that one could not see across them and, at the end of one such "great lake," an immense waterfall that literally shook the earth with its thunder. Could such prodigious natural wonders really exist? Believing so might have stretched Cartier's imagination to the breaking point, but Europeans would eventually see these things with their own eyes.

"The early explorers had an inkling there was this fantastic waterfall somewhere up along the St. Lawrence River," says Patrick McGreevy, author of *Imagining Niagara: The*

A View of ye Industry of ye Beavers of Canada in making Dams to stop ye Course of ye Rivulet, in order to form a great Lake, about wh they build their Habitations. To Effect this: they fell large Trees with their Teeth, in such a manner as to make them come Cross ye Rivulet, to lay ye foundation of ye Dam; they make Mortar, work up, and finish ye whole with great order and wonderfull Dexterity. The Beavers have two Doors to their Lodges, one to the Water and the other to the Land side. According to ye French Accounts.

Meaning and Making of Niagara Falls, which tells how perceptions of the falls have changed over the centuries. "They had heard rumors of it, but they had never seen it."

One of those who heard rumors of the falls was Samuel de Champlain, who during the early 1600s founded the colony of New France and the rustic outpost that would eventually become the city of Quebec. In an attempt to establish a profitable fur trade with interior tribes, Champlain journeyed far up the St. Lawrence and out onto Lake Ontario. He probably reached the far end of the lake, and on one of his maps he noted the approximate position of Niagara Falls. No doubt Champlain's American Indian guides described the great cataract to him and pointed to clouds of mist rising from the forests beyond the Niagara cliffs. If Champlain paid the falls a visit, however, he never said so in any of the seven books he wrote about his travels.

All of this was very early in the European experience with North America, and much of the seventeenth century would pass before a European explorer stumbled onto the falls and reported to the world what he had seen. Native Americans had been familiar with the falls for many centuries, if not thousands of years, but the European generally credited with "discovering" them is Father Louis Hennepin. A zealous young cleric, Hennepin joined the French adventurer La Salle on his late 1670s expedition to the heart of what then was still a very dark continent.

In November 1678 Hennepin and more than a dozen other members of the La Salle expedition set sail in a modest brigantine for the western end of Lake Ontario. La Salle had instructed them to blaze a trail through the Niagara country to the shores of Lake Erie. There they were to begin work on a stout little ship with which to explore the far reaches of the Great Lakes and trade for furs with the Indians. The initial leg of the journey almost ended in

disaster when the brigantine was caught in a blizzard on the open waters of Lake Ontario. Narrowly avoiding shipwreck by ducking into a sheltered bay near current-day Toronto, Hennepin and his half-frozen companions then pushed on to the mouth of the Niagara River, which they reached by early December.

When an attempt to advance up the river in a small boat was rudely repulsed by the strong current, the party set out on foot following an old American Indian portage trail. It led up the Niagara escarpment and around the raging rapids that had pushed them back. As they marched inland, a mysterious, deep-throated roar called to them from the forest. At first they tried to ignore it and press on toward Lake Erie, but the continuous booming—suggestive of distant cannon fire— grew louder and louder. Finally, their curiosity got the better of them. Turning toward the thunder, they hacked their way through walls of dense foliage until they emerged at the edge of a breathtaking chasm. There before them in all its wonder was Niagara Falls. They would spend the better part of a day marveling at a natural phenomenon unlike anything any European had ever seen, or even imagined.

Author Patrick McGreevy (above) says perceptions of Niagara have changed dramatically since explorer Samuel de Champlain (below) first heard rumors of the falls from the Indians. Devoted largely to beavers, the early seventeenth-century illustration (opposite) absurdly suggests the cataract may be half a league or roughly a mile high.

As a member of a missionary order known as the Récollets, Hennepin eschewed all possessions. Openly disdainful of the needs and desires of others less pious than he and firmly focused on the spiritual, he was not the sort of man to be very much impressed by things of this world. But Niagara Falls shook him to the core. Although weighed down with other seemingly more necessary equipment, Friar Hennepin carried a portable altar with him wherever he went. Upon sighting the falls, he set up his altar and began to pray.

"He was astonished," says McGreevy. "He later published an account of the experience along with a picture based on his descriptions that made Niagara Falls look maybe 600 feet high. For almost 150 years afterward, Hennepin's image of the falls would be the standard view of Niagara."

It was a dark and forbidding vision Hennepin gave the world, for rather than being

elated by what he saw, the friar was horrified. He described the chasm as a "dreadful gulf" and said that "one is seized with horror," to look upon the falls. He found he could not gaze at them for long without turning away. Perhaps this should not be surprising—the waterfalls Hennepin had seen in France were by comparison little more than country brooks obstructed by a few stray boulders. Niagara Falls was something altogether different. Standing at its brink, Hennepin must have felt very near the universal chaos, which he, with his mobile altar, so devoutly endeavored to avoid.

"Father Hennepin described it as a fantastic place where the unimaginable was possible," says McGreevy. "Many people thought that description applied to the New World as a whole. It was a place where things could happen that couldn't possibly happen in Europe. In the New World there was a Fountain of Youth, there were cities of gold, and there was—Niagara Falls. In this way the falls became a symbol, an icon for the New World."

Having survived his encounter with watery chaos, Father Hennepin packed up his altar and headed off to survey a very large expanse of a continent where the impossible seemed all too frightfully likely. First he helped build La Salle's trading vessel, a ten-ton bark christened the *Griffon*, then set sail with the explorer for the western lakes. The little ship would later vanish in a storm, but by that time La Salle and the intrepid friar had already disembarked and gone to explore the Mississippi River basin. Sent to locate the source of the Mississippi, Hennepin discovered the Falls of St. Anthony near present-day Minneapolis, but it was no Niagara. It did not capture his imagination or bring him to his knees in terror.

Eventually, Hennepin made his way back to Europe where, like Champlain before him and so many other explorers after, he published a detailed if somewhat fanciful account of his travels. Titled *Description de la Louisiane*, the book provides—even today—a thrilling read. Intending to give his readers a case of the shudders and, no doubt, to coax them to keep reading, Hennepin peppered his writing with words such as "frightful," "terrible," "horrible," and "abyss." In Europe, Hennepin's book transformed him from a penniless friar into a popular author. In North America, however, his overblown and more often than not inaccurate descriptions caused Hennepin to be regarded by historians and professional mapmakers alike as a spinner of gross exaggerations or—not to put too fine a point on it—a liar. Flawed though they may have been, Hennepin's descriptions stuck.

"Hennepin's image of Niagara is still not completely erased from people's minds," says McGreevy.

In fairness to Hennepin, there are those who visit the falls today and are deeply moved if not frightened by the spectacle of so much water rushing over a cliff. It has always been so. The falls are, after all, no minor creation of nature. When the Niagara River is running full tilt, more than 200,000 cubic feet of water—enough to float several vessels the size of the *Griffon*—plummet over the falls every second, so some hyperbole is to be expected.

Father Louis Hennepin and his companions discover Niagara Falls in a 20-foot-wide Thomas Hart Benton mural (opposite). The historic illustration above depicts construction of La Salle's Griffon on the shores of Lake Erie, southwest of the falls (below).

"Early maps of the Americas often had a picture of the falls in one corner," says McGreevy. "Mapmakers put it there as an example of the wonders that existed beyond the more 'ordinary' world of Europe."

For those who wished to see and experience those wonders for themselves, Niagara Falls was invariably a priority destination. "People have always wanted to come here," says McGreevy. "Niagara Falls has this aura about it, particularly for people from far away. When they think of North America, Niagara Falls comes to mind as one of three or four places they absolutely must visit."

But for centuries it was not an easy place to reach. "For most, it was all but inaccessible," says McGreevy. "People knew about Niagara Falls, but they couldn't get to it. This continued to be the case well into the nineteenth century. People might make a voyage to America and a trip to the falls perhaps once in their lives—for some, that may even be true today."

Uphill in a Canoe

Indian nations as a rule are always a prime target for land acquisition in the United States and in Canada, but our people see the land as priceless. It has no dollar value because it's irreplaceable. All of nature has a special meaning to our people. For myself, I only see power, strength, and unmatched beauty in the falls.

—Eli Rickard, Tuscarora Tribe

Early explorers such as Cartier, Champlain, and La Salle recognized the St. Lawrence River as a portal to the North American interior. But those who hoped to use it as a liquid highway to gain access to the vast resources of the continental heartland must have felt cheated by nature. At Quebec the broad St. Lawrence, many miles wide at its mouth, narrowed so dramatically that the passage upriver became much more difficult and dangerous. Rapids at Montreal made further progress next to impossible for large vessels, and an even nastier surprise lay at the far end of Lake Ontario, where a massive stone escarpment blocked the path of mariners. To reach the upper lakes and the rich, beckoning lands of the Midwest, one first had to find a way around Niagara Falls.

The Iroquois and other Native American peoples had long had a means of bypassing the falls, but it was a laborious one. Indian traders knew that the only way to move goods and materials from Lake Ontario to the shores of Lake Erie or the reverse was to carry the cargo overland on their backs. This is precisely what they did, often lugging their heavy canoes along with them. Their shuttling back and forth eventually beat down the thick foliage near the Niagara River, creating a distinct portage trail. It was this trail that La Salle and Hennepin used during the winter of 1678–79 to reach Lake Erie and begin the expedition that would eventually lead them to the mouth of the Mississippi.

The French were thus the first Europeans to recognize the importance of Niagara as a gateway to the upper lakes and the vast region beyond. The upper lakes could also be reached via the Ottawa River and a series of portages leading to Georgian Bay, but Niagara was nonetheless of immense strategic value. It was inevitable then that nations would fight for control of this geographic fulcrum.

Before the arrival of the French, various Native American nations warred with one another over the narrow neck of land separating the two lakes. By the time the French reached Niagara, the Iroquois were in ascendancy. Relations between the French and the five nations of the Iroquois Confederacy were frequently hostile, especially with the Senecas, westernmost of the tribes. When open warfare between the Senecas and the French broke out in 1687, the Marquis de Denonville, the governor of New France, ordered construction of a fort near the mouth of the Niagara River in an attempt to protect the portage and strengthen the French claim on the area. Under almost constant siege by the Senecas and racked by disease and hunger, the fort's hundred-man garrison had dwindled to only twelve by the time a relief ship arrived in spring. Soon afterward the fort was

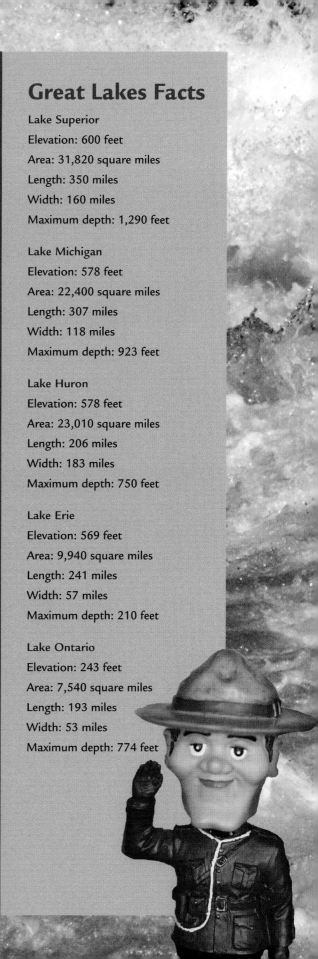

Great Lakes Facts

Lake Superior
Elevation: 600 feet
Area: 31,820 square miles
Length: 350 miles
Width: 160 miles
Maximum depth: 1,290 feet

Lake Michigan
Elevation: 578 feet
Area: 22,400 square miles
Length: 307 miles
Width: 118 miles
Maximum depth: 923 feet

Lake Huron
Elevation: 578 feet
Area: 23,010 square miles
Length: 206 miles
Width: 183 miles
Maximum depth: 750 feet

Lake Erie
Elevation: 569 feet
Area: 9,940 square miles
Length: 241 miles
Width: 57 miles
Maximum depth: 210 feet

Lake Ontario
Elevation: 243 feet
Area: 7,540 square miles
Length: 193 miles
Width: 53 miles
Maximum depth: 774 feet

abandoned, and three more decades would pass before the French were able to solidify their hold on Niagara.

In 1726 the French established a stronger fortress high on a bluff near the mouth of the Niagara River. Consisting of a stone barracks surrounded by a wooden stockade, it looked more like a frontier trading post than a military base. To encourage this impression, the French told local Iroquois peoples that it was the "House of Peace," and in time it came to be known as Fort Niagara. The fort saw little or no fighting until 1759, when the British invaded Canada in an attempt to bring the French and Indian War (1754 to 1760) to a close. By this time the stockade had given way to stout stone walls, but they could not hold back the British forever. After a nineteen-day siege, Fort Niagara fell, and loss of this strategic outpost hastened the defeat of the French at Quebec and elsewhere. Within a year the French were forced to cede all their North American possessions.

As it turned out, the Senecas were no happier with British incursions onto their lands than they had been with those of the French. The British saw the Niagara portage as a key bottleneck in the 1,000-mile-long supply line they used to support their settlements and military posts in the West. In 1761, to speed the movement of arms, provisions, and trade goods between the lakes, they placed an efficient pioneer by the name of John Stedman in charge of the operation. Known officially as "Master of the Portage," Stedman made a number of improvements. Most notable among them was the introduction of horse-drawn carts and covered wagons to carry cargo up the escarpment and along a crude but passable road. Previously, local Indians had performed this service for pay. Now they were unemployed—and angry.

At about this time, the great Ottawa chief Pontiac was urging Native American peoples throughout the Midwest to reclaim their ancient birthright and drive the white man off their ancestral lands. Local Seneca braves—many of them former porters—heeded Pontiac's call and soon began to harass Stedman's wagon drivers. To protect the drivers and their cargoes, Stedman organized armed convoys.

On September 14, 1763, Stedman led one such convoy southward toward Lake Erie. Rattling along the cliffs above the Niagara Gorge, the convoy had reached a dome of rock known to the Senecas as "Devil's Hole," when Stedman and his drivers heard an earsplitting war cry. Flaming arrows and musket fire cut down most in the convoy before they could defend themselves. Riding at the head of the wagon train, Stedman was able to speed away and escape with his life. Having roused British troops at Fort Schlosser not far from the falls, Stedman dispatched a small force to drive off the attackers and save the convoy. Instead, the relief column itself was ambushed and wiped out. Several days later, a larger British contingent reached the site of the battle. There they found no fewer than eighty bodies, but the death toll had obviously been much higher—many of the hapless drivers and would-be rescuers had been pitched into the gorge.

Rather than drive the British away from Niagara, the battle led to a substantial reinforcement of garrisons in the area. These strongpoints would play important roles, not just in further conflicts with the Indians but also in the Revolutionary War, which began barely a dozen years after the Seneca victory at Devil's Hole.

During the late 1770s, many loyalists in New York and Pennsylvania fled westward and sought the protection of the small British garrison at Fort Niagara. Rallying around John Butler, a staunch Tory, a group of these refugees formed a militia known informally as Butler's Rangers. The Rangers launched devastating raids deep into Continental territory, burning crops and settlements and interrupting the supply lines of the Continental Army. In time, however, it became apparent that neither the determination and grit of loyalists nor the combined might of British land and naval forces could prevent the thirteen rebellious colonies from establishing their independence. When the Treaty of Paris brought an end to the war in 1783, former Rangers and other loyalists founded the town of Niagara, now known as Niagara-on-the-Lake, Ontario. Placed by treaty on the east side of the newly drawn border between the United States and Canada, Fort Niagara eventually became a U.S. military post.

The War of American Independence was long past by 1812, when North Americans were swept up in what was essentially a European upheaval—the Napoleonic Wars. Ironically, on June 26, 1812, when word arrived in Niagara that war had been declared, British general Isaac Brock was entertaining a number of U.S. Army officers at Fort George just across the river from Fort Niagara. The general and his guests respectfully bid one another good evening and good luck in the coming conflict. Not all those who had dinner

Tuscarora: The Sixth Iroquois Nation

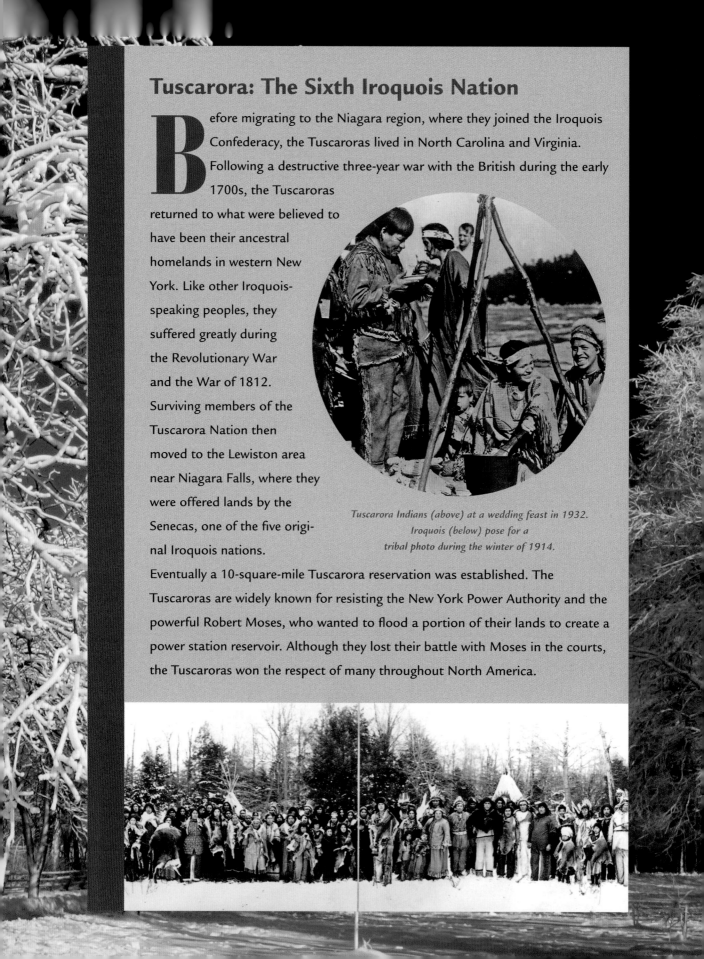

Before migrating to the Niagara region, where they joined the Iroquois Confederacy, the Tuscaroras lived in North Carolina and Virginia. Following a destructive three-year war with the British during the early 1700s, the Tuscaroras returned to what were believed to have been their ancestral homelands in western New York. Like other Iroquois-speaking peoples, they suffered greatly during the Revolutionary War and the War of 1812. Surviving members of the Tuscarora Nation then moved to the Lewiston area near Niagara Falls, where they were offered lands by the Senecas, one of the five original Iroquois nations.

Tuscarora Indians (above) at a wedding feast in 1932. Iroquois (below) pose for a tribal photo during the winter of 1914.

Eventually a 10-square-mile Tuscarora reservation was established. The Tuscaroras are widely known for resisting the New York Power Authority and the powerful Robert Moses, who wanted to flood a portion of their lands to create a power station reservoir. Although they lost their battle with Moses in the courts, the Tuscaroras won the respect of many throughout North America.

together that night would survive the war. Brock himself would be struck down by a musket ball during a momentarily successful U.S. cross-river assault on Queenston Heights. The British soon recaptured the heights, and for two years thereafter the fighting surged back and forth across the Niagara and along the shores of Lakes Ontario and Erie. Thousands on both sides would die in a war that in the end would accomplish nothing and change little.

After the war a flood of settlers poured into the Midwest, and as commerce increased, more and more wagons rolled over the portage road. Ships bringing cargo to the north end of the portage originally found their way to the mouth of the Niagara by following the plumes of mist rising from the distant falls. By 1780, however, they were guided into port by a light. Unlike most maritime beacons, which shine every night, this one was lit only when a vessel was expected.

Early photographs of Fort George showing Canadian troops at drill (above top), blockhouses (above lower), and a monument to those who served here.

During the 1820s, U.S. maritime authorities improved on this arrangement by establishing at Fort Niagara an official, full-time lighthouse with a resident keeper. Its light shone from a tower on top of the old stone barracks, which would come to be called the "French Castle." By that time, however, the days of the Niagara portage were numbered. The completion of New York's Erie Canal in 1825 and Canada's Welland Canal just four years later allowed commerce to reach the upper lakes without surmounting the Niagara Escarpment. Even so, freighters and other vessels occasionally approached Niagara, and the lighthouse was always there to guide them.

During the 1870s, U.S. maritime authorities decided Fort Niagara needed a still better lighthouse and ordered construction of a 60-foot-tall limestone tower capped by a metal and glass lantern room. Focused by a polished glass lens, the light shining from the tower served ships on storm-tossed Lake Ontario right up until 1993, when it was replaced by a modern beacon. Resembling the turret of a medieval fortress, the old tower still stands and is a frequently visited attraction of the Niagara Falls area.

Wonder of Wonders

Entirely beyond the Ordinary

We do hear a lot of comments from the passengers about the power and the glory and that sort of thing, but I see it more from Mother Nature's point of view. Geologically speaking the falls are a bit of a fluke because the rock formations have allowed them to maintain their shape over thousands of years rather than turning into a series of rapids. But, yes, it is hard to come here, see the falls, and not marvel at the wonder of it all.

—*John Williams, captain,* Maid of the Mist

While the Niagara Escarpment represented both a commercial opportunity and a strategic bottleneck that several nations thought worth spilling blood for, the grand waterfalls it had spawned were something altogether different. Their appeal was a spiritual one, or so it seemed at first. Like Friar Hennepin, most early European visitors had a peculiar reaction to the falls. They were afraid of them, as if they had seen in the cataracts a clear reflection of God Almighty or of a different sort of deity they had no words to describe.

"This was a waterfall completely unlike anything Europeans had ever seen or imagined," says Elizabeth McKinsey, author of *Niagara Falls: Icon of the Sublime*. "Many of the early depictions of the falls show little people standing at the brink and gesticulating wildly. Sometimes they're cowering or they've fallen to the ground because they simply can't face it any longer. Some people said they could hear the voice of God calling to them from the falls."

If the falls were intimidating, even terrifying, they were also powerfully alluring and attractive. Everyone wanted to see them with their own eyes.

The Maid of the Mist *approaches the American Falls, Goat Island, and the serpentine Cave of the Winds stairway.*

During the 1820s the falls were circumvented by Canada's Welland Canal (below) and New York's Erie Canal, opened by governor DeWitt Clinton in a ceremonious "Wedding of the Waters" (right).

"It was a place entirely beyond the ordinary world," says author Patrick McGreevy. "It was an icon for the New World, and many people thought of taking a trip to Niagara Falls as a kind of pilgrimage—something they should do at least once, something that would perhaps change their lives."

During the eighteenth and early nineteenth centuries, getting to Niagara might very well change a person's life—or end it. This was no easy destination to reach. In 1800 the journey from New England took weeks of bone-jarring carriage travel followed by many days of arduous and, all too often, dangerous hiking. Around the falls, wolves and rattlesnakes were plentiful.

Those who wished to climb down into the gorge had to descend along a series of notched logs, using scrawny vines as handholds. In 1785 French writer, intellectual, and world traveler François-René de Chateaubriand considered himself lucky to have survived the descent with no injuries more serious than a broken arm. Thirty years later, a local entrepreneur built a spiral staircase that allowed the adventurous to go exploring behind the falls.

If you went, you got a certificate, but the walk was treacherous. All the more so, one visitor noted, because of "the number of small eels twisting about under your feet in all directions."

"Part of the initial appeal of Niagara was the fact that it represented untouched virgin American wilderness" says McKinsey. "But of course, it would not stay that way. As more people came to this area, the whole area became settled and built up."

A tidal wave of change was washing westward across North America and, inevitably, Niagara was swept up in it. On November 4, 1825, the governor of New York poured a keg of water from the Great Lakes into New York Harbor to celebrate the completion of the Erie Canal. Only four years later the locks of the Welland Canal in Ontario would likewise swing open as a whole new web of canals and roadways linked East to West as never before. The continent was shrinking, and the frontier was steadily retreating in the direction of the setting sun. The great western adventure was transforming the country, and soon it would be whacking up wide rivers with steamboat paddle wheels and chugging swiftly west on the wheels of the new steam-powered railroads.

The effect of all this on Niagara Falls was to create the world's first great tourist resort. People who had decided not to move west with the pioneers could instead come to Niagara on holiday. If Niagara was not the wild and boisterous frontier, it was nonetheless a darned fine imitation.

Quick to cash in on a good thing, local businessmen opened hotels, inns, restaurants, and saloons. They built fences to protect the view of the falls from their own properties or to cut off the view from others. They were snake oil salesmen peddling an elixir of real value— a natural wonder so inspiring that it could revive the spirit or touch the soul.

The Erie Canal: New York's Artificial River

Early settlers who wished to tap the immense resources and development potential of the North American interior were confronted by a formidable mountain barrier. In Canada the Laurentians and in the United States the Adirondacks and Appalachians made transportation and commerce between East and West extremely difficult. The St. Lawrence and the Hudson were the only major navigable rivers that penetrated the great wall of mountains, and neither of them provided ready access to the West.

In the late eighteenth century, European nations had solved similar transportation problems by building canals fitted with locks that enabled vessels to be raised up and over obstacles. Usually these canals consisted of a series of segments that could be closed off, or "locked," and filled or drained as needed to lift or drop boats and ships to the desired level. Climbing from one lock to the next as if up or down a staircase, canal boats and other vessels could safely and efficiently gain or lose hundreds of feet in elevation as they made their way along the canal.

New York politicians and businessmen thought such a system might enable boats to reach the upper Great Lakes by way of the Hudson River and the Mohawk River Valley. However, everyone recognized that building the canal would be no minor undertaking. More than 363 miles of highly varied terrain separated Lake Erie from Albany, where the Mohawk flows into the Hudson. To reach the lake, westbound boats would be forced to climb 568 feet, a seemingly impossible feat that, in the end, would require more than eighty locks.

Dismayed by the enormity and high cost of the project, President Thomas Jefferson turned it down flat, as did the New York State Legislature. In 1817 a business-minded visionary named DeWitt Clinton became governor of New York, and he soon secured the necessary funding from the state legislature. Construction of the canal occurred under the supervision of James Geddes and Benjamin Wright, a pair of state judges with no previous experience in engineering. To design the canal and its critical system of locks, Clinton hired Canvass White, an amateur engineer, and Nathan Roberts, a mathematics teacher and land speculator. Together these men came up with a workable plan calling for a shallow canal that could accommodate barges up to 7 feet wide, 61 feet long, and with a 3.5-foot draft. Elevation gain or loss would be accomplished in 12-foot steps by way of locks that were 90 feet long, 15 feet wide, and able to hold two boats at a time.

Construction began in 1817 on what quickly came to be called "Clinton's Ditch," but progress was slowed by dense forests and hardpan so tough that it bent shovels and dulled picks. Two years were required to complete a single 96-mile section from Rome to Utica. Tragedy struck when hundreds of workers died of "swamp fever" in the marshes west of Syracuse, and yet work continued.

By 1823 more than 250 miles of canal had been finished, linking the Hudson River with Rochester on Lake Ontario. Two years later the canal reached Lake Erie at

Buffalo, completing a task that had once seemed impossible. Governor Clinton celebrated the event by pouring a keg of Lake Erie water into the Hudson River, a symbolic act he described as a "Wedding of the Waters." The mountains had been surmounted and East tied to West once and for all.

For almost a century, mules pulled grain- and coal-laden boats along the Erie Canal, which was finally replaced by the New York State Barge Canal in 1918. A distinct canal-boat lifestyle developed along the Erie. It is recalled today by some U.S. elementary school students, who sing the Erie Canal folk song, with its chorus: "Low bridge, everybody down; / Low bridge, for we're comin' through a town."

The Flying Schooner of Niagara Falls

When you work down here every day, day after day, and see all the water that's coming over the falls and never stops, it sort of reminds you of the people lining up for the boat and the tourists who just keep coming and coming, same as the water.

—*John Williams, captain,* Maid of the Mist

The first visitors to Niagara Falls were caught up in the wonder of it as a phenomenon of nature. Phenomena can be magnificent, wonderful, even awe-inspiring, but spectacles are *thrilling.* During the early nineteenth century, the interest in Niagara Falls as a phenomenon began to be replaced by the realization that it could be exploited as a money-making spectacle. Some who came here looked upon the falls and, instead of beauty, saw a vision of dollars and cents raining down in an endless torrent. They only needed to hold out their hats to catch a fortune. The carnival of exploitation began, it can be said, on September 8, 1827, with the last voyage of the sad ark called the *Michigan.*

By the mid-1820s unscrupulous promoters had begun to crowd out less greedy Niagara innkeepers and business owners while squabbling among themselves over every scrap of land with a view of the falls. When their investments returned disappointing profits, they argued, ironically, that nature was to blame. Nature was no longer popular—no longer the attraction they needed to bring in visitors and separate them from their money. What they required instead was showmanship.

William Forsyth and John Brown, a pair of rival Canadian hotel owners, are said to have hatched the scheme. Forsyth and Brown had fought in the courts—and some believe with their fists—over access to a popular falls viewing area. They tore down each other's fences and ripped up each other's plank walkways. They shouted and squabbled. But when it came to promoting local tourism and cashing in on the same, they were of a single mind. It was a simple idea really: They would send a ship over the falls and invite the world to come and watch.

"The hotel owners advertised," says Paul Gromosiak, a historian and author of nine books about Niagara Falls. "They said, 'Come and see a ship go over the falls loaded with wild creatures.'"

Their broadside read in part as follows:

> The Pirate, MICHIGAN, with a cargo of ferocious animals will pass the GREAT RAPIDS and THE FALLS of NIAGARA, 8th September, 1827, at 3 o'clock. The Michigan has long braved the billows of Erie, with success, as a merchant vessel; but having been condemned by her owners as unfit to sail . . . her present proprietors, together with several public spirited friends, have appointed her to convey a cargo of Living Animals of the Forests . . . through the deep rolling rapids of the Niagara, and down its grand precipice into the basin *below*. . . . The greatest exertions are being made to procure Animals of the most ferocious kind, such as Panthers, Wild Cats, Bears, and Wolves; but in lieu of some of these, which it may be impossible to obtain, a few vicious and worthless Dogs . . . and perhaps a few of the toughest of the Lesser Animals will be added to and compose the cargo. . . . Such as may survive and be retaken, will be sent to Museums at New York and Montreal, and some perhaps to London.

The vessel chosen for this spectacular, one-way journey was a derelict lake schooner with the faded letters MICHIGAN on her bow and stern. For many years the *Michigan* had shuttled passengers, lumber, and whatever other cargos her owners could muster for her from one Lake Erie port to another. Her life shortened by hard use and the even harder midwestern weather, the leaky old schooner was abandoned and might in time have rotted down to the waterline had she not come to the attention of Niagara Falls promoters. Forsyth bought the *Michigan*, had her patched up just enough to stay temporarily afloat, and then gaudily decked her out as a pirate ship, no doubt complete with Jolly Roger.

Historian Paul Gromosiak (above) recounts the schooner Michigan's plunge over the falls, an 1820s publicity stunt. Decades later the steamer Maid of the Mist (opposite) took a more dramatic—and certainly more heroic— journey through the Niagara Gorge.

On the night of September 7, the *Michigan* docked beside the ferry landing above the falls, where curious visitors were charged an admission to board and examine her. Those who paid probably did so in hopes of seeing the fierce creatures that were supposed to have been onboard, but if so, they were disappointed. Despite the claims made in advertisements, the living cargo assigned to the *Michigan* consisted of a single pathetic dog, two raccoons, a few geese, a small bear, and a buffalo.

"These were the *wild animals* they put on board," says Gromosiak. "I'm sure the poor things were terrified. But people came to see this. They flocked along the shores of Goat Island and the mainland to see the *Michigan* go over."

The throng attracted to this bizarre spectacle was indeed enormous. On the day of the event, crowded passenger steamers arrived from Lake Erie with brass bands playing gaily on their decks. Wagons rattled in from rural areas loaded with farmers and their families. Hucksters sold cake and beer or relieved the gullible of their hard-earned money with games of chance. As many as 15,000 spectators—the largest crowd that, up to that time, had ever assembled at Niagara—looked on from the shores when at last the *Michigan* was towed out into the middle of the river and consigned to her fate.

Bridal Veil (left) and Luna Falls tumble from the edge of Goat Island in Niagara Falls State Park. The Cave of the Winds stairway (lower right) carries visitors to within a few feet of these spectacular cataracts.

Drifting steadily toward the rapids and the falls beyond, the schooner must have been a very strange sight indeed. The Stars and Stripes flew from the *Michigan*'s bow, the Union Jack from her stern. Stuffed effigies dressed in pirate garb took the place of living sailors, none of whom would have been stupid enough to make this voyage. The animals were caged or tethered to the deck and so had no choice but to take the plunge along with the doomed *Michigan*. One exception was the bear, which having broken free, very sensibly mutinied from the vessel's unwilling crew and jumped over the side. Struggling valiantly against the current, the bear managed to reach shore safely, but these exertions proved to have been in vain. No sooner had the hapless creature clambered onto dry land than it was shot dead.

"They should have treated that poor animal as a hero," says Gromosiak. "Instead, they shot it."

Meanwhile the *Michigan* was spinning around, crashing into rocks along the length of the rapids, and falling apart. Her masts were gone by the time she reached the crest of Horseshoe Falls, where she broke in half and fell in pieces over the edge. Just before the *Michigan* reached bottom, people saw one of the geese take wing and fly away. None of the other animals onboard were ever seen again.

As it turned out, the stunt proved an astounding success. Every hotel in the area had been filled for days. Every ounce of liquor and morsel of food on hand was sold at respectable prices. Fortunes were made, and Niagara Falls was changed forever.

Suspended by Steel Ropes

It was the beginning of the industrial revolution, and there was a great lament over the loss of the natural world. Poets and artists saw America as the last vast wilderness, but the domination of nature and of native peoples had become part of the idea of manifest destiny. It had come to be seen as progress.

—*Jolene Rickard, Tuscarora Tribe*

As settlers poured westward past the falls, the interior of the continent began to open up, and dependable transportation was needed to tie the new farming communities in the Midwest with markets in the East. Coaches, wagons, and canal barges could carry heavy loads, but they moved along at the pace of a plodding mule. Development lagged because getting from one place to another took far too long. However, travelers and shippers could soon rely on a speedier beast of burden—the iron horse.

By the 1840s railroad tracks connected thousands of cities, towns, and villages. To accomplish this miracle of linkage, the ubiquitous ribbons of steel had slashed their way through dense forests, crossed vast prairies, and scaled lofty mountain ranges, but even the most ambitious railroad men were intimidated by some of these obstacles. One of these was the mighty gorge carved out by the Niagara River after it plunged over the falls. A breathtaking chasm some 800 feet wide and 200 feet deep, it was long believed to be entirely beyond the skills of bridge builders.

Then two fast-growing rail lines blew into Niagara: the New York Central and Canada's Great Western. Their locomotives chugged almost to the rim of the gorge, close enough for their passengers to see smoke rising from the stacks of engines on the other side of the gorge. Without a bridge, this was as close as the tracks of the two railroads could come. But businessmen on both sides of the falls were eager to bring the two lines together, a coupling they reckoned would unleash a flood of tourists and tourist money.

How could this be done? The swirling waters down in the gorge were a very unfriendly place for bridge supports. The river channel above the falls was little more promising, and any bridge built there would surely detract from Niagara's legendary scenery—the very reason tourists wanted to come here in the first place. Clearly an innovative approach was required. Fortunately, the mid-nineteenth century was an era alive with fresh engineering concepts such as the suspension bridge. Builders had learned that modest spans could be suspended from two or more supports with rope, but these were mostly small rural bridges

Completed in 1855, John Roebling's beautiful and technologically advanced suspension bridge used spun-wire cables to hold the structure aloft.

and certainly not strong enough to carry heavy rail traffic. Made of hemp or other vegetable fibers, rope was weak, and under sufficient strain it would invariably unravel and snap. Then a German-born engineer named John Roebling thought of replacing the hemp with wound bundles of wire, and the steel cable was born.

In 1846 Roebling had used his cables to construct a stout, 1,500-foot-long bridge across the Monongahela River at Pittsburgh. Some believed a similar technique might work at Niagara, but ironically, when the railroads decided to move ahead with the project, Roebling was not chosen to design the new bridge. Instead, that honor went to the young, ambitious Charles Ellet Jr., who had studied bridge building in France and attended the prestigious École Polytechnique in Paris.

Ellet designed a structure not unlike the one Roebling had built over the Monongahela. A suspension bridge held aloft by cable, its 800-foot central span would be 25 feet wide—enough to hold a standard-gauge railroad track and accommodate two-way carriage and pedestrian traffic as well. Located 2.5 miles downstream from the falls, it would feature a panoramic view of both the American and Horseshoe Falls and so provide a completely new way to enjoy the world's premier natural wonder. All this he offered for what seemed a bargain-basement price of $190,000, and he promised to have the bridge completed and open to traffic in time for the 1849 summer tourist season.

Impressed with Ellet's grand design, the railroads commissioned the project. Construction was scheduled to commence early in 1848, but before work could begin, it was necessary to get a line across the gorge. Ordinarily the line would have been ferried across the river by boat, but the torrential Whirlpool Rapids blocked any such attempt.

"They couldn't do it in the traditional way because of the rapids, the 200-foot Niagara Gorge, and the whirlpool," says Buffalo's Meg Albers, an expert kite flier who is more familiar than most with this particular page of Niagara history. "They considered a steamship, a cannon, even a bow and arrow, but none of this would work."

Ellet briefly considered using a rocket, but he finally settled on a low-tech approach. The innovative, first-of-its-kind Niagara suspension bridge project would be launched not with a blast or a bang but with the gentle whisper of a northwesterly breeze. The line would be carried across the gorge by a kite.

A small prize was staked for the first kite flier skilled or lucky enough to get a line over. Dozens of young boys vied for the cash, but none accomplished the feat until fifteen-year-old Homan Walsh sent aloft a homemade kite he called "the Union." Crossing by ferry to the Canadian side of the river to take advantage of the prevailing winds, Walsh kept his kite aloft all day and into the night, playing out hundreds of feet of cord. Then, around midnight, the wind died. He had almost succeeded! Walsh's kite drifted lazily to the earth on the far side of the gorge, but the string, having lost its tension, dropped into the chasm, where it caught on a rock and snapped.

"It was January, and the ferries had stopped running because of ice in the river," says Albers. "Walsh was stuck on the Canadian side with his kite down in the gorge."

The ice jam lasted for eight days, leaving Walsh marooned in Canada, where he relied on the hospitality of Canadian friends for his room and board. Finally the ice cleared, the ferries resumed operation, and Walsh was able to get back over to the U.S. side and retrieve his kite. Eager to make another attempt, he crossed back to Canada and sent the Union skyward once again.

"This time it worked!" says Albers. "The Union was caught on the far side."

Workers used the intact string to pull across a stronger cord. That, in turn, was used to pull over a still heavier line, followed by a stout rope. In time a wire cable made its way across, and construction of Niagara's suspension bridge was at long last under way.

The determined Ellet pushed his workers hard, and by July they had spanned the gorge with a narrow service bridge. Although work on the railroad bridge had barely begun, the service bridge was itself a considerable achievement. Now for the very first time, ordinary people could walk across the Niagara Gorge and see the falls as few had ever seen them. Many were willing to pay for the privilege, and Ellet collected thousands of 25-cent tolls. No doubt this would have been seen in a very favorable light by Ellet's employers—if the builder had not decided to keep all the money for himself. The railroad owners believed the tolls were rightfully theirs. The squabbling over these initial revenues grew so intense at one point that Ellet warned railroad officials away from the bridge with a cannon loaded with buckshot. Perhaps not surprisingly, rather than the cannon, Ellet himself was fired. When he countered with a lawsuit, the railroads paid him $10,000 to quit the project without further litigation.

To replace the troublesome Ellet, railway officials turned to none other than John Roebling, whose so-called "wire rope" had made the bridge possible in the first place. Work did not begin again until 1851, but once under way, it moved ahead at a steady pace. Even so, it would take more than four years to complete.

Roebling supervised nearly every aspect of construction, immersing himself in the project so thoroughly that he was often aware of little else. When his wife bore him a son at their Trenton, New Jersey, home in January 1854, Roebling was notified of the event in a business letter from an associate. Some say he was puzzled at the news, since he had forgotten she was pregnant.

Opened to the public on March 18, 1855, the Roebling Bridge was quite different from the one Ellet had envisioned. It had two tiers instead of one and, more significantly, was more or less rigid in design. Hung from four cables, each spun from 3,640 separate wires, it weighed more than 1,000 tons. Unlike many other suspension bridges, this hefty structure was not susceptible to the violent swaying and vibrations that doomed many similar structures. Regardless of ice, wind, or weather, it could carry heavy freight trains while standing as steady as the rocks on either side of the Niagara Gorge. Roebling's Niagara Bridge lasted for forty-two years and was finally retired to make way for a larger structure. By contrast, a suspension bridge Ellet built across the Ohio River stood for less than five years before it succumbed to high winds in 1854, only months before Roebling's span carried its first trains.

The delightful Donna Marie Campbell painting (above) shows youngsters trying to win a cash prize by flying a line across the Niagara Gorge. Winter ice bridges like those in front of the old incline railway (opposite) sometimes made it possible to walk across the gorge.

A modern freighter descends the Welland Canal's stair-step locks.

Sailing through Pastures: The Welland Canal

Cartier, Champlain, La Salle, and other early European explorers understood that an efficient water route would be needed to tap the rich agricultural and mineral resources of the North American interior. The Great Lakes seemed to offer such a route, but an important link in the chain of lakes was broken by the Niagara Escarpment, which blocked ships with a wall of rock more than 300 feet high. For centuries the only way around this barrier was an overland portage linking Lake Ontario with the upper Niagara River and Lake Erie. With completion of New York's Erie Canal in 1825, however, the Niagara obstacle was finally surmounted.

Work on the Erie Canal had begun in 1817, and as it progressed, Canadians became increasingly concerned over the likely loss of commerce to U.S. business interests once the canal was finished. As a result, in 1824 Canada launched its own canal project, headed by William Hamilton Merritt, a St. Catharines merchant who was no less a visionary than New York governor DeWitt Clinton, who had launched construction of the Erie Canal. Known as the Welland Canal, Merritt's new artificial waterway sought to bypass Niagara Falls by way of Twelve Mile Creek and the Welland River. Between the creek and river, a series of locks would stair-step vessels over the Niagara Escarpment.

Although it was less than one-tenth as long as the Erie Canal, building the 27-mile Welland Canal took nearly five years. Much of that time was spent on the canal's forty locks, each of them 110 feet long, 22 feet wide, and 8 feet deep. On November 27, 1829, the Welland Canal opened to barge traffic, and there were now two water routes to the West. While the two canals were in competition, agricultural production in western states and provinces grew so fast that there was always plenty of business for both. Even the coming of the railroad, which began to crisscross Canada and the United States during the late 1820s and 1830s, did little to stem the flow of goods and produce through the canals.

The lake schooner York *passes through a Welland Canal lock in 1840.*

Although the Welland Canal saw heavy traffic, the private company that operated it was never profitable. The Welland Company found that it could not charge tolls high enough to cover the high cost of maintaining the wooden gates of the canal locks. The company lost money constantly until 1839, when the Government of Upper Canada agreed to buy it. In time the troublesome locks were replaced by new masonry structures capable of handling cargo-laden sailing ships. The first steps had now been taken along a path that would eventually turn interior lakeside cities such as Detroit, Windsor, Chicago, and Thunder Bay into seaports.

Still a key segment of the modern St. Lawrence Seaway, the Welland Canal has been rerouted, enlarged, or otherwise improved a number of times. In 1887 a new canal was dug to straighten the Welland and open it to deeper draft vessels. It had locks 270 feet long, 45 feet wide, and 14 feet deep. Beginning in 1913 the canal was deepened and enlarged again, and by the time this renovation was completed in 1932, Welland locks were nearly three times as large as they had been twenty years earlier. Today, Welland locks are 766 feet long, 80 feet wide, and 27 feet deep. Even so, ships have grown so much larger over the years that only freighters of relatively modest size can use the canal and, thus, the fabled St. Lawrence Seaway.

Daredevils

Blondin and Farini

You don't really give much thought to the danger that's involved, although maybe the tourists do. For them it's part of the show they've come here to enjoy . . . just like in the old days with the tightrope walkers . . . they'd lower things down to the *Maid of the Mist*, and one guy even climbed down to the boat on a rope.

—*John Williams, captain,* Maid of the Mist

The first time he laid eyes on the yawning gorge below Niagara Falls, Jean Francois Gravelet made up his mind to walk across it on a wire. This was no ordinary ambition, but Gravelet—a muscular French acrobat who went by the stage name of "Blondin"—was no ordinary man.

"Blondin was the world's greatest high-wire walker—maybe the greatest who ever lived," says Shane Peacock, a noted author and playwright from Thunder Bay, Ontario, who has written extensively on high-flying, wire-walking daredevils like Blondin. His book *The Great Farini: The High-Wire Life of William Hunt* is considered among the most revealing works on the subject.

"He was very elegant on the wire," says Peacock. "You might say he was the Mozart of the high wire."

Like all professionals who have become the best in their field, Blondin sought the ultimate challenge, and at Niagara he thought he had found it. He was already world famous by the time he first visited the falls in 1858 at the age of thirty-five, but fame and fortune were not everything to a man of Blondin's drive and ambition. He soon became obsessed with the notion of carrying his act out over Niagara's roiling chasm.

"Blondin said he had a dream about the falls," says Peacock. "In this dream he had seen himself walking over Niagara Falls on a silken cord."

The following summer Blondin returned and took the walk for real. Well publicized, the event attracted a crowd of 25,000

Although dim and blurry, this 1860 photograph captures the breathtaking spectacle of a Farini ropewalk across Niagara Gorge with American Falls roaring in the background.

Charles Blondin crosses the gorge with his ever-trusting business manager on his back. As the broadside (opposite) suggests, Blondin also made the crossing while tied in a sack.

spectators—an enormous throng for the era—and Blondin put on quite a show for them. The mere sight of the blond, handsome, goateed acrobat was enough to make ladies swoon; and when he inched out onto his wire, some of them literally fainted. The entire crowd was soon giddy. Once he had gotten well out over the chasm, where he was beyond all hope of rescue and sure to die should he falter, Blondin did what no one had expected. He began to dance. He jumped high in the air. He even turned somersaults. Once he reached the far side of the gorge, Blondin haughtily turned and retraced his steps. The roar of approval that rose from the huge audience drowned out the thunder of the falls.

"You have to remember that nobody had ever done this before," says Peacock. "People were amazed that you could even put a wire across the gorge. It was considered a stunning feat of engineering. And then to actually get on it and walk across it made Blondin seem a superman."

During the days leading up the event, spectators who had arrived early got a much different impression of the performer. They had watched him ride out over the gorge in a small cable car to check his wire—actually a rope made of Manila—for stability. At one point he stopped the car and got out to take a few practice steps and turn a somersault. Then he sat down on the wire as if to relax and eat his lunch. Blondin, the death-defying high-wire walker, was thus seen in a slightly less superhuman light—as Jean Francois Gravelet, the highly professional showman.

No doubt, many of the thousands who turned out a few days later to view his crossing were unaware of Blondin's skills and fully expected him at some point to pitch head first into the river and be killed. If so, they were disappointed. Blondin not only completed his round-trip journey over the Niagara Gorge but also repeated the performance several more times that summer. Each of Blondin's wire walks attracted a massive crowd of spectators willing to pay 25 cents to watch, but to keep them coming he had to continually retool his act. He did handstands on the wire; he balanced on a chair; he crossed the gorge blindfolded; he pushed a wheelbarrow over the wire; he lay down on the wire as if to take a nap; he took his walk dressed in a monkey suit. Finally, having seemingly emptied the well of theatrical stunts, he even carried his ever-trusting business manager over the gorge on his back.

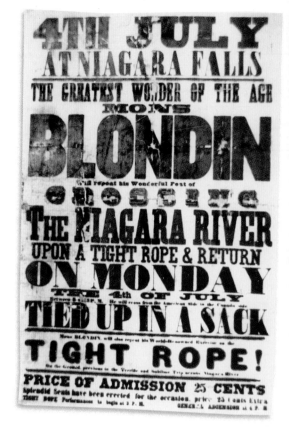

Blondin's feats made headlines around the world, and one of those who read about him in the papers was a southern Ontario farm boy by the name of William Leonard Hunt. Pointed by his father toward a career in medicine, Hunt quickly became bored with his studies and opted for a life as a showman instead. Practicing acrobatics, he learned to walk a rope in the family barn. He also became incredibly strong. It is said he could lift up to 700 pounds. Invited to perform at a local fair, Hunt thrilled crowds by standing on his head on a rope stretched across a river. Soon after, he changed his name to Guillermo Antonio Farini, which he felt had an exotic, show business ring to it. All this got him kicked out of the house by his father who, until then, believed he had raised a country doctor.

Believing he had no place to go but up, the inexperienced Farini set out for Niagara in 1860 to challenge the best in the business. Blondin, who at this point had never heard of Farini, had every intention of building on his triumphs of the year before with a series of return performances during Niagara's summer tourist season. This time, however, Blondin found that he had competition—and from a man with a real flare for business.

Farini had watched one of Blondin's performances early in the summer of 1860 and afterward amazed his friends by bragging that he would equal or better the Frenchman's feats. Within two months he had made good on the boast. On August 15, 1860, Farini crossed the gorge on his own tightrope. Not only did he match most of Blondin's previous feats, but he also lowered himself by rope to a boat in the river.

The vessel in question was the *Maid of the Mist,* and at its helm was Joel Robinson,

The Great Farini hangs by the knees before shimmying down a vertical tether to a boat more than 150 feet below. Blondin (opposite) cooks dinner while suspended above the Niagara River.

who just one year later would pilot the *Maid* through the Whirlpool Rapids in a wild daredevil exploit of his own. Robinson held the boat steady as Farini dropped like a huge spider onto the deck, where he toasted the passengers and the amazed audience up on the cliffs with a glass of champagne.

Having finished his wine, Farini then calmly grasped the rope and began an arm-over-arm ascent to his wire more than 100 feet overhead. He had not practiced the climb, and it proved far more difficult than he had expected, so much so that the stunt almost cost the young showman his life. A wind blew up, causing the rope to pendulum back and forth through the gorge and draining his arms of all their strength. Soon his arms and shoulders were numb, and the only feeling left in his hands was pain. The exhausted performer only just managed to clamber back atop the wire and continue with his act. Although nearing the point of collapse when he reached the far side of the gorge, Farini resolved to make the return trip as Blondin had done and as he had promised to do in his advertising circulars. After just ten minutes of rest, Farini set out again; awhile later he reached the other side— blindfolded and wearing baskets on his feet.

Farini's performance was distinct from Blondin's in one very important way. Farini had arranged beforehand for $1,000 bonuses from the railroads and for a percentage of the receipts from excursion boats on the river. Counting the proceeds from ticket sales to as many as 40,000 spectators, Farini turned a profit of more than $9,000 on the venture. This was far more than Blondin had ever earned for any of his wire walks, and the Frenchman was incensed.

"Blondin didn't like this very much because he considered Niagara his own personal show," says Peacock.

Blondin was sure he could outperform his inexperienced competitor, but it was not to be. Every stunt Blondin concocted, whether it be carrying volunteers across the gorge on his back or walking the wire while stitched up in a sack, Farini matched or surpassed. While he could not equal Blondin's grace or acrobatic skill, Farini never lacked for strength or guts, and he invariably used these qualities to impress and awe his crowds. The high-wire rivalry careened queasily onward before reaching what most observers agreed was a stalemate toward the conclusion of the 1860 tourist season. By that time it had progressed from the merely pointless to the purely ridiculous.

"Blondin decided to carry a stove across Niagara Falls," says Peacock. "So he put the stove on his back, walked halfway across the gorge, and cooked himself some eggs."

Farini countered by doing his laundry.

"Thinking he had to do something even more extraordinary, Farini went out and got himself a washing machine, put it on his back, and carried it out there over the gorge," says Peacock. "When he was about halfway across, he lowered a bucket all the way down to the river, pulled it back up by rope, and washed his clothes."

Most believed the competition would continue the following year and likely end with the death of one of the two performers. As it turned out, neither man would wire-walk

the Niagara Gorge again. In 1861 the American Civil War shut off the flow of tourists to Niagara Falls, and attentions turned to dangers and demonstrations of valor far more meaningful than those exhibited above the Niagara Gorge.

By 1861 Blondin had carried his act and his recently acquired American wife, Charlotte, to England, where he put on a special performance at the Crystal Palace by request of the Prince of Wales, who had seen one of his shows at Niagara Falls the previous

year. Afterward, Blondin settled his family into a comfortable suburban London estate, which he called his "Niagara Villa." The name was fitting, since the worldwide acclaim Blondin earned at Niagara had made him a rich man. In just two seasons he had piled up a fortune of more than $400,000. Although officially retired, Blondin continued to perform in venues on both sides of the Atlantic until the age of sixty-eight. His last high-wire performance was

given at Belfast, Ireland, in 1896. Five years later he died peacefully in his bed, having fallen not from any of the great heights he had challenged but to diabetes.

During the Civil War, Blondin's former competitor, Farini, served briefly in the Union Army. In 1864 he turned up in Niagara again, telling lurid tales of cloak-and-dagger spy adventures behind Confederate lines. He also claimed to have invented a sort of pontoon shoe that would allow soldiers to literally walk across the water. Supposedly he had personally demonstrated his floating shoes for Abraham Lincoln. To this day, no one is sure whether any of these outlandish stories were true. Likely, as with the dangers Farini had faced during his high-wire performances, they contained elements of both truth and illusion.

That same year, Farini attempted one more amazing Niagara stunt—trying to walk on stilts to the edge of American Falls. The performance collapsed when one of his stilts broke, leaving him injured and stranded for several hours on a small island in the middle of the river. Help could have reached him much sooner, but nearly everyone believed that his seeming plight was merely part of his act. Eventually it became obvious that Farini was in real trouble, and a party of rescuers plucked him from his rock and brought him safely ashore.

In the years that followed, Farini went back on the wire—though not at Niagara Falls—and thrilled crowds as never before. He organized a circus and took it on tour around

the world. He learned seven languages and
became an expert in horticulture. He wooed and
married a German aristocrat, a niece of Richard
Wagner. When he could no longer perform, he
picked up a brush, became an artist, and won
awards for his canvases. It seemed that in nearly every endeavor, he was a success. Outliving
Blondin by more than thirty years, he witnessed the dawning of a whole new era with its airplanes, radios, and automobiles, things that neither he nor his audiences could have imagined
way back before the Civil War. Still, despite all he had seen and done in a life that extended to
1929, when he died at the age of ninety-one, the focal point of his existence would remain
those few golden weeks in 1860 when he had gone toe-to-toe with the greatest high-wire performer in the world.

More than a few wire walkers would follow in the footsteps of Blondin and Farini at
Niagara. In 1873 Henry Bellini drew large crowds to his walks on a heavy, 1,500-foot-long
rope stretched near the American Falls. Although born in England to Italian parents, Bellini
billed himself as the "Australian Blondin," a moniker he had picked up after a successful performance below the equator. Bellini was able to duplicate nearly every one of the feats
accomplished by Blondin and Farini. In fact, he outdid them with one amazing stunt. He
leapt from his rope into the river more than 100 feet below, breaking his fall with a rubber
tether that he released at just the right moment. On another occasion, Bellini was nearly
killed when the tether got tangled around his feet. He never repeated the stunt.

Apparently Bellini was jealous of his abilities and quick to anger. When Stephen Peer,
one of his assistants, attempted an impromptu rope-walking performance of his own, an
enraged Bellini tried to cut the rope. Undeterred by this nearly fatal assault, Peer went on to
become a professional performer in his own right. He died under mysterious circumstances

after a rope walk over Whirlpool Rapids in 1887. Some believed that Peer, by that time known by the stage name Professor Peere, had been murdered. Others claimed he had accepted a drunken dare, tried to walk across the gorge in the dark, and fell off the wire. His crushed body was found on some rocks beside the river.

Not all the Niagara wire walkers were men. In 1876 Italian performer Signorina Maria Spelterini crossed the Niagara Gorge repeatedly on an 800-foot rope much like the one Blondin had used. Sometimes she made the crossing blindfolded, or with peach baskets strapped to her feet.

In all, more than a dozen wire walkers would try to recapture the magic of 1860, but they would not succeed. Like Bellini, they could repeat or even surpass earlier feats, but they were competing against not men but legends. As the years went by, their names—Bellini, Peer, Spelterini, Dixon, Calverly, and others—would fade and be forgotten. But far into the twentieth century there were still oldsters who told their grandchildren and great-grandchildren that they had been there at Niagara in 1860 and seen the Great Blondin and Farini suspended in midair above the most awesome chasm on the planet.

Over the Falls in a Barrel

I guess some people are thrill seekers, and they just want to try something crazy—go over the falls in a barrel, kayak, a Jet Ski, or something like that. I'm a bit of an adrenaline junkie myself, so I can kind of relate to it, but I would never try anything like that.

—*John Williams,* captain, Maid of the Mist

If truth be told, many of the thousands who came to see Blondin, Farini, and others walk across the Niagara Gorge on shaky ropes and thin wires paid their good money in hopes of witnessing a tragedy. They wished no ill, but if these performers were hell bent on committing suicide in so spectacular a manner, then they might as well be on hand to watch them fall into the river. The wire walkers never obliged their thrill-seeking fans in this way, for the dangers they flirted with were more apparent than real. However, a wholly different and far more dangerous variety of death- and nature-defying stunt would come to the falls in the new century.

It was a simple idea, really. Instead of dancing on a wire and chancing a fatal fall, these twentieth-century stunters would actually take the plunge. Having crammed themselves into a barrel or some other floating conveyance, they would drift out into the Niagara River, shoot the rapids, and be swept over the falls. With luck—quite a lot of it—they would survive. Without luck, well, at least they would get their names in the newspapers.

Incredibly, the first to attempt this seemingly crazy feat was a sixty-three-year-old woman. Annie Edson Taylor, a former dance instructor from Bay City, Michigan, had fallen on hard times. She had grown too old and overweight to attract paying students. Taylor lived in an era when society was rigidly divided into haves and have-nots, and she was definitely one of the latter. There was no Social Security or other public programs that might help her, so Taylor was forced to rely entirely on her own wits and daring—and of the latter she possessed an abundance.

It was 1901, and the Pan-American Exposition had focused the attention of the world on Buffalo and nearby Niagara Falls. With tens of thousands attending the big fair, daredevils attempted to cash in by drawing crowds with a variety of harebrained stunts. For instance, on July 11, with the fair in full swing, Carlisle Graham survived a wild and nearly fatal ride in a metal drum through the Whirlpool Rapids a few miles below the falls. Graham had performed earlier Niagara stunts, but because of the fair, this one was widely reported in newspapers. When Taylor in Bay City read of his exploit, a light went on in her head. Three months later she turned up in Niagara Falls with a large oak barrel.

Armored with numerous iron hoops, Carlisle Graham's elongated barrel carried him safely through the violent Whirlpool Rapids about 3 miles below the falls.

"Taylor was desperate to make money so that she wouldn't end up poor in her old age," says author Paul Gromosiak. "She decided to go over Horseshoe Falls. She would be the first to do it."

The months leading up to Taylor's arrival had not been without drama. A vaudeville performer named Martha Wagenfuhrer had followed up on Graham's exploit with a similarly violent passage through the rapids—in the very same drum, in fact—and lived to tell the tale. Wagenfuhrer's stunt took place on September 6, a date laden with dark irony. President William McKinley had traveled to Buffalo to attend the exposition and had just toured the falls. McKinley may have briefly considered remaining in Niagara to watch Wagenfuhrer's spine-jarring ride, but if he did, he rejected the idea in favor of an affair in the Temple of Music at the exposition. There a twenty-eight-year-old self-styled anarchist by the name of

A color image showing a replica of Annie Taylor's barrel is superimposed on a 1901 photograph of the aging teacher being helped ashore by onlookers after she survived her reckless plunge over Niagara Falls. Later Taylor took her barrel on tour (see opposite) but earned little from the venture.

Leon Czolgosz stepped from a long reception line and, instead of taking the president's hand, stuck a pistol to his chest and fired two shoots. A few days later McKinley died, leaving the ship of American state in the bully hands of Theodore Roosevelt.

Even more ominous from Taylor's point of view was an event that took place the day after the McKinley shooting. Another woman tried to run the rapids, this time with fatal results. The stunt called for young Maude Willard, a burlesque performer and friend of Wagenfuhrer's, to race through the rapids in a wooden barrel accompanied by her pet fox terrier. The by-now experienced stuntman Graham was supposed to swim alongside Willard's barrel, but swirling waters quickly separated him from it. Graham completed his swim through the pounding rapids, but the barrel got caught in the vortex of the whirlpool. By the time it was retrieved several hours later, Willard had suffocated. The fox terrier survived.

If there had been reason to believe that Graham, Wagenfuhrer, or Willard might survive their stunts, there seemed no hope whatever that Taylor would live through the ordeal she had in mind. While they had limited their activities to the rapids below the falls, Taylor intended to ride her barrel over the Horseshoe Falls themselves and into the churning maelstrom below. It was a drop of more than 180 feet, and most reckoned that, even if it did not shatter the barrel, the impact would surely kill her.

"To think of some woman in her sixties getting into a barrel and going over Horseshoe Falls," says Gromosiak. "No one had ever done that before. It certainly took a lot of courage—or else she was not exactly all there."

Indeed, many at the time thought Taylor might not be entirely sane. Others looked upon her stunt as a bizarre form of suicide. All believed she would be killed, but though some tried, nobody could convince her to abandon the project.

Finally, October 24, the day of the big event, came, and the old woman crawled into her barrel, which she had named Queen of the Mists. Braced with heavy iron hoops, the unlikely craft appeared stout enough even if its passenger seemed fragile. The barrel was fitted with pillows for padding and a sort of harness to provide her with a modicum of protection from the impact and the violent buffeting sure to follow.

Once inside the barrel she complained that it was leaking. The assistants she had hired with what little money she could raise told her not to be concerned about the leak—

that the whole thing would be over long before the barrel took on any significant volume of cold river water. No doubt they thought that the leak was the least of her worries.

The local police were convinced of the suicide theory concerning Taylor's stunt and made a halfhearted attempt to stop it. To avoid them, her assistants pushed her bobbing vessel out into the river about a mile above the falls. The Queen of the Mists moved slowly at first, but it soon was gripped by the full force of the current. Grating over shoals and slamming into rocks, it swept forward with a breathtaking inevitability. Taylor heard a roar, at first distant but growing more thunderous by the second. Then came an instant that few others could imagine and that she would never forget. Later she described it as a sense of personal obliteration. Indeed, she felt that "all nature was being annihilated."

She had gone over the edge.

Taylor noted no appreciable impact as the Queen of the Mists struck the water at the foot of the falls. Rather, she was aware of being sucked beneath the surface. Perhaps a minute passed before the battered barrel and its badly shaken passenger emerged from below and shot some 15 feet into the air. Minutes later they had been pulled ashore. Someone took the top off the barrel, and a man shouted.

"The woman is alive!"

Annie Taylor had gone over the falls, but the event produced neither her death nor the happier ending she had envisioned. She had planned to take her barrel on tour and, billing herself as the "Heroine of Horseshoe Falls," make a good living by entertaining audiences with the story of her adventure. As it turned out, she had a very dull and boring stage presence, and her drowsy audiences grew increasingly small. Finally, she was reduced to selling postcards on the street and ended her days in just the sort of place she had risked her life to avoid—a poorhouse.

Taylor may have been the first, but she was certainly not the last to brave the falls in a padded barrel or some other such contraption. "She was followed by at least fifteen other people," says Gromosiak. "They went over in pickle barrels, truck tire inner tubes, heating tanks, rubber balls, and steel drums."

In 1990 there was even a kayak. "The young kayaker said he was going to make it, and maybe he believed that," says Gromosiak. "He even had dinner reservations for later that day, thinking he would have no problem keeping them. The kayak was recovered, but they never found poor Jessie Sharp.

"And then in 1995 we had Robert Overacker from California, who wanted to draw attention to the plight of America's homeless veterans by taking on the falls on a Jet Ski. His parachute was supposed to open up when the Jet Ski went over. It didn't. He dropped like a rock and was killed."

Over the years, however, most who have taken on the falls have done so in barrels. Among the barrel riders was Bobby Leach, the first man to survive a ride past the lip of Niagara Falls, that gut-wrenching point where Annie Taylor said she sensed the imminent destruction of the entire natural world. An experienced professional stuntman who had been a performer in the Barnum and Bailey Circus, Leach took his trip over the falls in 1911. He went on to make better business use of the experience than had the less savvy Taylor. Even so, his life ended, as hers had, in an ironic, even pathetic manner. While touring with a burlesque troop in New Zealand, he slipped on an orange peel and died from his injuries.

The old postcard above celebrates the feat of Martha Wagenfuhrer, who shot the rapids below the falls in 1901. The image opposite shows Carlisle Graham's barrel tumbling through the rapids, also in 1901. In 1911 Bobby Leach (below) spilled over the falls in a bullet-shaped iron tank.

Niagara attracts all sorts of daredevils, such as Jay Cochrane (above) in a recent wire walk. Barrel rider Karel Soucek (below) survived a well-publicized trip over the falls in 1984, only to be killed in a later stunt at the Houston Astrodome. George Stathakis died during a 1930 plunge in his aptly named Death Barrel (opposite). The interior of the barrel hardly looks comfortable.

"Not a banana peel, mind you, an orange peel," says Gromosiak. "He ended up in the hospital with gangrene in his leg, and he died from that. So Leach had gone over Horseshoe Falls and survived, then slipped on an orange peel and died."

Yet another barrel rider was George Stathakis, likely one of the strangest individuals to test his luck against the falls. The forty-six-year-old Stathakis made the trip in 1930 in a massive barrel made of staves 4 inches thick. He took with him "Sonny Boy," his pet turtle, said by Stathakis to be one hundred years old. Stathakis explained to the press that should he himself not survive the experience, then Sonny Boy would be left to tell them all about it. Perhaps Stathakis had a premonition, since the turtle survived and he did not. Adopted by the Niagara Falls Museum, Sonny Boy lived on for many years after his plunge over the falls.

"The turtle never said a darned thing to anyone," says Gromosiak.

A flurry of barrel riders took on the falls during the 1980s and 1990s, and more have followed since.

These latter-day stunters have made the trip in crafts very unlike the simple oak cask that Annie Taylor rode into legend in 1901. Most have been equipped with elaborate if not high-tech safety features to increase the odds of survival, and a few have even included hammocks, oxygen tanks, and radios. No matter how well designed the so-called "barrel," however, success is not guaranteed.

In 1984 Canadian Karel Soucek took the big drop in a converted metal oil drum fitted out with a padded bucket seat, lights, and a radio transmitter. Completed without serious incident, Soucek's stunt was recorded by a professional film crew for publicity purposes. Ironically, Soucek was killed the following year while re-creating the stunt before a crowd in the Houston Astrodome.

Why did they do it, and why do they continue to do it? Although the rewards have been almost invariably disappointing, many, like Taylor, went over the falls to make a name for themselves and to make money. Others, like Stathakis, may have been a touch deranged. Likely as not, however, most really didn't know why they decided to take the world's greatest and most dangerous thrill ride.

Festival of Light and Dark:
Pan-American Exposition of 1901

Intended to celebrate the progress of civilization and the growing technological and economic power of the Americas, Buffalo's Pan-American Exposition turned out to be one of history's most memorable world's fairs. Spread across more than 340 acres in the northern reaches of the city, the fairgrounds were opened by Vice President Theodore Roosevelt on May 1, 1901. Before the exposition closed six month later, it had attracted more than eight million visitors and been touched by a tragedy of historic proportions.

Interestingly, exposition promoters wooed paying customers with brochures that all but ignored the city of Buffalo and instead highlighted the widely recognized symbol of the New World—Niagara Falls. Not surprisingly, many thought the fair was actually being held beside the falls. Despite any confusion, however, the millions who attended the exposition were in no way disappointed—it delighted them with an unheard-of array of sights, sounds, experiences, and exhibits. A Grand Canal, an impressive selection of art and music halls, a lively carnival-style midway, and an assortment of "villages" supposedly depicting the lives of Eskimos, Mexicans, Africans, and Native Americans forced visitors, who could not possibly do or see everything, to make difficult choices. To highlight the exposition's focus on technology, an Electric Tower was illuminated each night by thousands of colored lights. The latter exhibit emphasized the exposition's strong link to Niagara Falls, where hydroelectric plants generated the power used at the fairgrounds.

Today the exposition is perhaps remembered less for its future-oriented design and exhibits as for a pair of gunshots that were destined to echo throughout the nascent century. President William McKinley had been slated to open the exposition in May, but because of scheduling conflicts he sent Roosevelt in his stead. Little more than four months later, the president would finally make his fair appearance. There, on September 6, following an all-day excursion to Niagara Falls, McKinley was gunned down by anarchist Leon Czolgosz. Eight days later the president died from his wounds at the home of prominent Buffalo resident John Milburn. Not long afterward Roosevelt—in town to be near the rapidly failing McKinley—was sworn in as the twenty-sixth president of the United States.

MAY 25 1901   PRICE TEN CENTS
COLLIER'S
PAN-AMERICAN EXPOSITION
EDWARD PENFIELD

An admission ticket (facing page) provided access to many exposition wonders such as the brightly lit Temple of Music (opposite) and Electric Tower (right). No doubt many visitors bought souvenir posters like the one above.

Reserved *and* Sacred

Frederic Church's Cathedral

If you come later in the day when the sun is in just the right place, you get better rainbows.

—*John Williams, captain,* Maid of the Mist

As the first railroads chugged into Niagara, they brought with them a flood of tourists. Once considered a sublime natural wonder, the falls were opened to exploitation of every sort. But more than a few who stepped down from the passenger cars at the Niagara Falls terminals were looking for something more than cheap thrills. Their attitude toward the falls and toward nature in general was quieter and more respectful—reverent, in fact. To them the key to true spirituality lay in a deep appreciation of nature.

"Niagara Falls attracted romanticists because it was supposed to overwhelm your emotions," says author Patrick McGreevy. "It was a place not for rational calculation but rather for a sort of spiritual rapture."

Launched in Europe during the first quarter of the nineteenth century, the romantic movement was typified by the likes of Samuel Taylor Coleridge, whose verses extolled nature, and Ludwig van Beethoven, whose exuberant symphonies lifted emotions to unexpected heights. The movement found expression not just in literature and music but in the visual arts as well.

A rather late disciple of the romantic movement, which began to give way to Victorianism about the middle of the nineteenth century, was Frederic Edwin Church. A New England landscape painter, Church had honed his skills under the tutelage of Thomas Cole, a founder of the well-known Hudson River school of artistry, which sought to unveil nature's spiritual underpinnings. In 1856 Church began to make sketches of what is arguably the most romantic natural phenomenon in the world—Niagara Falls.

"I observe the courses of the river and all the glories

Among the most popular attractions at the falls are the rainbows that streak the mist with color on sun-lit days. Frederic Edwin Church included a rainbow in his 1850s masterpiece depicting the falls.

offered to my view," said Church. "I lose myself in unbounded space. I am nothing. God is everything."

In all, Church would make three trips to Niagara, examining it from many angles and taking advantage of every available viewpoint. The photographic process was quite new to the arts at that time, but Church had experimented with it and used it to make him a better observer. His eye became a camera lens and his mind, the film, but he remained as ever a brush, canvas, and easel artist, not a photographer. Driven by his passionate desire to *reveal* the falls rather than merely *depict* them, Church produced dozens if not hundreds of drawings. With these in hand, he returned to his home on the Hudson and set to work on what most consider his masterpiece.

"Church's 1857 painting is *the* masterpiece of Niagara Falls, pure and simple," says author Elizabeth McKinsey. "The colors are vivid. Church could see the falls as if he were seeing it through binoculars. He could see the vastness, but he also painted the details. Compositionally, his great breakthrough was to eliminate the foreground. There is no ground

Niagara (1857), Frederic Edwin Church's famous painting of Horseshoe Falls. The artist provided no foreground, leaving viewers visually adrift in the canvas as if they were about to be swept over the brink.

for the viewer to stand on in that painting. It's as if you're standing in the water just a few feet from the brink."

Nearly 8 feet wide and 3 feet high, the canvas is of respectable size, and almost all of it is taken up by the waterfall itself. There are few if any unnatural intrusions, since Church left out buildings and all but a mere hint of human figures. The water seems in constant motion, and it glows with an inner luminance.

Mid-nineteenth-century American art critics agreed that they had never seen anything quite like it. The painting created a stir from the moment it went on display in New York on May 1, 1857. It was purchased for $4,500—a stupendous sum at the time and one that helped make Church one of America's most prosperous artists. The buyers, the New York art firm of Williams, Stevens, and Williams, recouped their investment many times over by selling reproductions, which were snapped up by the thousands. An art critic described the painting—not the falls themselves, mind you—as the "eighth wonder of the world."

"This painting resonated with Americans," says McGreevy. "It was like a flood that washed away the past and washed away Europe. Seeing it, Americans felt like they were coming down from Noah's Ark at the end of the biblical flood into a fresh world where they could start over."

Just as does the story of Noah, Church's painting of Niagara Falls features a rainbow. It fascinated the famous English critic John Ruskin when he first saw the canvas on display in London. At first, Ruskin wasn't even sure the rainbow was part of the painting.

"Ruskin thought the rainbow must have been created by light passing through a nearby window," says McKinsey. "So he put his hand between the window and the painting to see if the rainbow would vanish. It didn't."

Clearly, Church had accomplished something new and exciting. He had done what others thought was impossible—captured on canvas a living waterfall.

"Niagara Falls was a huge challenge for artists from the beginning because they felt it was beyond their power to paint," says McKinsey. "It was elemental water, atmosphere, rock, and motion, whereas by definition a painting is static. It was a challenge that artists kept trying to meet but felt they really couldn't. Church was the one who, it was said, *came, saw, and conquered*. Interestingly, this language of conquest was actually used by art critics and others at the time."

Church's painting represented the joy of discovery in a virgin land. That at least was the romanticists' view of the painting and of Niagara Falls itself, but it was not the only view. Ironically, at the time Church was completing his painting of the falls, romantic adoration was already beginning to give way to other attitudes toward nature. Nature was chaos. Nature was frightening. Nature had to be challenged and somehow controlled. As we shall see, many during the late nineteenth century believed that Niagara Falls not only could, but should be conquered—even if that meant destroying it.

Nature's Architect

This is a very powerful place . . . a spiritual place . . . that needs to be respected . . . and needs to be seen as more than just a tourist destination.

—*Jolene Rickard, Tuscarora Tribe*

Frederic Edwin Church's great painting *Niagara* is remarkable not just for what he captured on canvas—the true magnificence of the world's premier natural wonder—but also for what he left out. By the middle of the nineteenth century, much of the *wonder* and nearly all the *nature* at Niagara Falls had vanished. It had been replaced by a tawdry assemblage of cheap hotels, sawmills, factories, carriage stands, curio shops, gaming parlors, and taverns. Lining both sides of the Niagara River, they had all but obliterated the view and left little here for a refined or sensitive observer to appreciate.

"It is difficult to imagine such ugliness as one sees on this small belt of land," wrote one disheartened visitor. Indeed, exploitation and development had so blighted Niagara that some travelers stopped considering it a worthwhile destination.

"Many people who came to Niagara went away disappointed," says McKinsey. "They'd seen all the gift book images, the prints, and the paintings, and they'd read the hyperbolic descriptions. Then they got here and said, 'Oh, is this all there is?'"

Frederic Church knew there was more— much more—and he had painted it. Another who saw not what Niagara Falls was but what it *should be* was Frederick Law Olmsted. Born in 1822 in Hartford, Connecticut, Olmsted had more

Landscape architect Frederick Law Olmsted struggled for decades to save what was left of the falls and make it part of a two-nation "Niagara Reservation" for use as a nature park open to all.

or less invented the art and profession of landscape architecture. During the 1850s he had designed New York's famed Central Park, and he would later design the grounds for the White House and the U.S. Capitol in Washington, D.C.

In 1864 President Abraham Lincoln had appointed Olmsted to a commission organized to establish and administer the pristine federal lands that would eventually become Yosemite National Park. In that capacity, Olmsted articulated a philosophy that still guides the National Park Service to this day. He believed that the people of an increasingly urban and industrialized world needed parks that put them in touch with nature and afforded them "the greatest possible contrast" with their day-to-day lives in the city. City dwellers occasionally needed to restore themselves with a tonic he described as "tranquillity," and this could only be found in nature.

Olmsted had these concepts in mind one warm August afternoon in 1869 when he took a stroll with two friends on an island in the Niagara River. His companions that day were powerful men who shared his views on modern life and the need for nature parks. One was William Edward Dorsheimer, an influential politician from Buffalo; the other was noted New York City architect Henry Hobson Richardson. Certainly there was little enough tranquillity to be found along the raucous and overdeveloped banks of the Niagara, but the three friends came upon just what they were looking for on Goat Island out near the middle of the river.

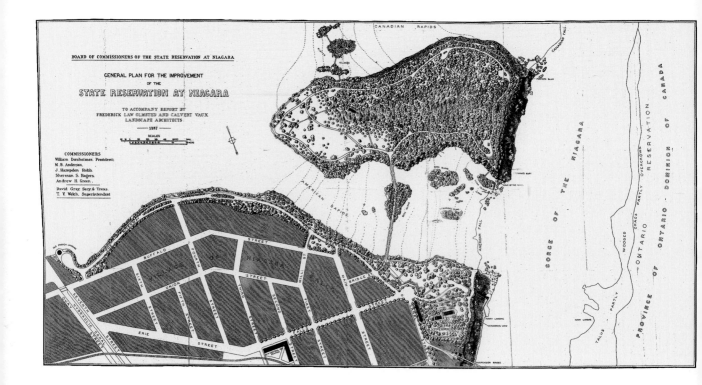

BOARD OF COMMISSIONERS OF THE STATE RESERVATION AT NIAGARA

GENERAL PLAN FOR THE IMPROVEMENT
OF THE
STATE RESERVATION AT NIAGARA

TO ACCOMPANY REPORT BY
FREDERICK LAW OLMSTED AND CALVERT VAUX
LANDSCAPE ARCHITECTS
1887

COMMISSIONERS
William Dorsheimer, President;
M. B. Anderson,
J. Hampden Robb,
Sherman S. Rogers,
Andrew H. Green,

David Gray, Secy & Treas.
T. V. Welch, Superintendent

This 1880s map was part of Olmsted's General Plan for the Improvement of the Niagara Reservation. The map shows Goat Island, American Falls, and the New York bank of the Niagara River.

Since Goat Island was hard to reach and a poor site for construction, it had been left more or less as the early explorers had found it. The island's tangle of lush vegetation resisted their progress, but eventually the three reached the falls and were rewarded with a view not unlike the one that might have been witnessed by Friar Hennepin two centuries earlier. By the time they had returned to the mainland, Olmsted had conceived what many at the time considered a bizarre, if not altogether impossible dream—he would find a way to sweep away the clutter of unsightly buildings and restore Niagara Falls to its original glory. What was more, he was determined to see the falls opened to all and its wonders preserved for the enjoyment of future generations.

Olmsted's plan unfolded slowly, for in those days attitudes toward nature were very unlike those of today. In 1869 pioneers were still trudging westward and clearing trees to make room for farms. A stump did not signal the loss of a tree but rather was seen as a sign of progress. Even so, Olmsted and more than a few others were beginning to have second thoughts about the way North Americans treated the land—indeed, about the entire human relationship to nature.

"There was this idea that you could connect nature and man and end up with a better life," says Tom Yots, the official town historian of Niagara Falls, New York. "That's what Olmsted and a lot of others thought. They were influenced by the romantic movement of the early nineteenth century, and they believed that nature lifted people's spirits and opened the way for them to improve themselves. That's why Olmsted created Central Park and the Buffalo park system."

Olmsted didn't just appreciate nature, he wanted to protect it, and Niagara Falls provided him with what was, perhaps, his most challenging opportunity to do just that. It fairly cried out for protection.

"Olmsted loved Niagara Falls," says Yots. "To him this was nature at its best."

However, the situation at Niagara was very different from the one he had encountered

in the nearly pristine Yosemite Valley. At Niagara, mere preservation was not enough. Here it would be necessary to turn back the clock.

"Olmsted had a very elite concept of Niagara," says Bill Irwin, author of *The New Niagara*, an engaging study of the impact of tourism and technology on the falls. "He wanted to make it a pure nature preserve. He wanted all human construction removed from the vicinity of the falls. He wanted people to appreciate nature for its own sake."

Of course, that's not what everyone who came to Niagara Falls wanted. The hotels, restaurants, shops, and saloons had sprung up because there were plenty of tourists willing to pay for such amenities, and likely as not, such people were more interested in the thrill of the falls than in its natural beauty.

"A lot of people just wanted the sensational," says Irwin. "This is what they had read about. This is what they expected."

Olmsted was rowing against the current, but he was a determined and persistent man. Waging a nonstop public-relations campaign that took nearly two decades, he refused to concede defeat. If his drive to preserve the falls were ever to be successful, however, he would need help, and he knew it. In 1878 the assistance he sought stepped forward in the person of Frederic Church. Coincidentally, Olmsted and Church were distantly related. They had many common acquaintances in New York City and elsewhere, but as it turned out, their most potent personal link was their mutual love of Niagara Falls.

Now world famous and lionized by the public for his depictions of the falls and other natural wonders, Church had many powerful friends, and he was able to convince officials in both Canada and the United States to take a new look at Olmsted's proposals. By 1885 governments on both sides of the river had made the substantial appropriations needed to buy sensitive acreage—some 520 acres in all—for a protected Niagara Reservation. Unnecessary structures were removed, and all lands adjacent to the falls and the islands in the river were opened to the public. Finally, after decades of wanton exploitation, the view of the falls was free to all.

It had happened. For the first time in the history of either the United States or Canada, public monies had been used to buy private land for the purpose of preservation. What is more, a worldwide conservation movement had been launched, one whose influence is still felt today and will be far into the future. Olmsted could not imagine a better place for this to have happened than at Niagara Falls.

"It is a spot reserved and sacred to what divine power has already put there," Olmsted wrote in triumph in 1887.

Not all his contemporaries agreed, however. Another point of view had taken root in America, and with it another plan for Niagara. This time the great goal was not to protect the waterfall, but to use it for something regarded as superior to mere scenery—a source of power. Many hoped to take the water out of the falls and harness its seemingly infinite power to light homes, brighten streets, and drive the gears of industry.

Niagara Parks Canada

When the Niagara Reservation was established in 1885, Canada set aside 154 acres (62.2 hectares) on the west side of the border to protect the area around Horseshoe (Canadian) Falls. Known today as Queen Victoria Park, this acreage is now only a small part of a much larger park complex encompassing several square miles of greenbelt, scenic roadway, and recreational trails. Stretching all the way from Lake Ontario to Lake Erie, these parklands provide access to what is probably the greatest single travel attraction on the North American continent—Horseshoe Falls. However, there are many other attractions, including the ever popular *Maid of the Mist* excursion cruises;

Whirlpool Aero Car, providing an extraordinary view of the rapids below the falls; Journey behind the Falls; Niagara Heritage Trail; Butterfly Conservatory; nature walks; and gardens.

The Canadian parks are administered and promoted by the Niagara Parks Commission, founded in 1887 not long after the Niagara Reservation was brought into existence. The commission is a self-funding enterprise similar to a private corporation but is responsible to the government of Ontario. The expenses of maintaining and protecting the commission parklands are paid from revenues and fees collected from the millions of visitors who enjoy the area each year.

In recent years the Niagara Parks Commission has undertaken extensive conservation and historical preservation initiatives. In 1995 Niagara Parks assumed control of the Chippewa Battlefield, where U.S. and British/Canadian armies met during the War of 1812. More than 800 men from both sides were either killed or wounded in this sharp engagement, now preserved by the commission.

To plan a trip, write Niagara Parks Commission, Box 150, Niagara Falls, Ontario, L2E 6T2, Canada; or visit the agency Web site: niagaraparks.com.

Water *into* Light

"Momma, I Bought the Ditch"

The early settlers came here because of the power potential. They looked at the falls and wanted to put the water to work turning mill wheels and producing things. At first the city was called Manchester, for Manchester, England, which was an industrial city, not a tourist city at all. In fact, up until the 1950s, tourism was always a secondary thing here.

—Tom Yots, Niagara Falls historian

The second half of the nineteenth century brought with it a bright new hubris. Stunning technological breakthroughs spawned a host of life-altering inventions such as the electric light, phonograph, and camera. Towering engineering marvels such as the Brooklyn Bridge and the Eiffel Tower suggested that humanity need no longer stand in awe of mighty natural phenomena. Nature could be controlled. Nature could be improved. Nature could be harnessed and made to serve human purposes. And nowhere did these notions pack more practical and symbolic punch than at Niagara Falls.

"Americans have this idea that their national values are reflections of the country's natural setting," says historian Bill Irwin. "At the same time, they see America as a technological nation."

Often the two concepts are not compatible. Strip mines and oil fields clash painfully with scenic wilderness vistas that might otherwise symbolize boundless opportunity and freedom. Similarly, turning off a mighty waterfall as if it were a tap that someone carelessly left running would surely destroy its capacity to inspire.

The awesome power of the falls may stun and inspire visitors, but when harnessed by hydroelectric plants, it can also light cities.

"These two ideas have been pitted against each other right here at the falls," says Irwin. "Almost from the first, Niagara Falls was a place where new technologies were tried out and progress was put on display. We've had world's fairs, model factories, electric power generation, and great bridge-building endeavors, and all these things were out there on the cusp. American progress seems to have gotten its foothold here at Niagara Falls, which is extremely ironic, since the falls are considered by many to be nature's greatest handiwork."

Technologists of the nineteenth century looked to the future and believed they could see utopia—an ideal society. Inventers, builders, and industrialists believed they could take creation into their own hands and make a better world—perhaps even a perfect world—if they could only get the necessary materials and energy.

"They came here and they saw the majesty of nature," says Irwin. "But they also saw Niagara as a tremendous opportunity. Here was all this horsepower just going to waste. Put it to work and they could not only solve problems but turn North America into a utopia."

Of course, all this was much easier to imagine than to accomplish. The Niagara River defied even the boldest plans to harness its power. Ironically, there was too much power

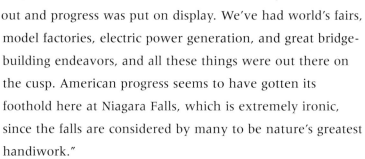

Augustus Porter (below) was among the first to make use of Niagara's water power, but his modest efforts tapped only a tiny fraction of the falls' nearly limitless energy potential, especially for electric power production. The early twentieth-century panorama above includes a hydroelectric plant and power lines.

here—far too much water, and it was moving far too fast. Exposed to the full force of the Niagara's current, old-fashioned waterwheels would be swept away in an instant, and no factory could stand for long at the brink.

Early-nineteenth-century Niagara settler Augustus Porter believed he could solve these problems by siphoning off just enough of the river's water. He built a canal some three-quarters of a mile long around the falls and used the water rushing through it to power a flourmill. A town grew up around the canal and the small industries spawned by the river and its fast-moving water. This in turn opened the area to travelers, and tourism became an important local industry in its own right. As a result, Porter was soon pouring much of his energy and capital into the construction of hotels and other facilities to make money from the tourists. A more comprehensive effort to take advantage of the Niagara's raw power would not be made until the late 1870s.

With only one customer, Porter's canal never made money, and by 1877 the company that ran it had filed for bankruptcy. The canal and surrounding property were put up for sale in an auction that attracted only a few bidders, most of whom were more curious than interested. After all, how much could a waterlogged trench be worth? To nearly everyone's surprise, a Buffalo businessman by the name of Jacob Schoellkopf stepped forward and offered $71,000 for the property and water rights. The relieved—and most likely astonished—auctioneer told Schoellkopf that the canal was his.

After the auction, Schoellkopf went home and crowed about the purchase to his wife. "Momma," he said, "I bought the ditch."

A man of daring and keen business sense, Schoellkopf understood what many did not, that bankrupt businesses were often gold mines in disguise—all they needed was a little know-how and determination to make them profitable. Having deepened and lengthened the canal, he installed turbines that turned the rushing water into power. Soon seven busy factories were running their machinery with power supplied by the canal. However, Schoellkopf had something even more audacious in mind.

In 1879 inventor Charles Francis Brush convinced a Cincinnati, Ohio, physician to let him string wires around the doctor's house. Brush hooked the wires to a generator and one of the electric-arc lamps he had recently designed, and presto, the house was all lit up! Kerosene lamps and gaslights would never look quite so bright again, and soon afterward Brush was erecting electric streetlamps in Cleveland and elsewhere.

These widely reported events did not escape Jacob Schoellkopf's attention. He began to see his canal investment and the Niagara's power potential in an even more positive light. Within three years he had built on the banks of his canal the world's first hydroelectric plant. The electricity it generated was used to power streetlamps in Niagara Falls, New York—and, for one shining season, to throw spotlights on the American and Horseshoe Falls. The lighting of the falls was seen as cause for an enthusiastic celebration featuring, of all things, a torchlight parade. Hordes of curious visitors came to Niagara on trains, not to see the falls but to witness firsthand the miracle of electric light.

Observing all this, knowledgeable engineers shook their heads in disdain. They saw Niagara's puny hydroelectric plant and streetlamps as mere curiosities more useful for attracting tourists than for improving the day-to-day lives of people. They recognized that Schoellkopf's canal tapped only a tiny fraction of Niagara's vast well of power. It taxed their patience to see the remainder wash over the falls and "go to waste," but putting all that water to work would not be easy. It would require herculean feats of engineering and construction and would touch off a titanic struggle between two of the greatest geniuses of modern times.

Battle of the Electric Titans

I do not hope that our children's children will ever see the Niagara cataract.

—*Lord Kelvin, nineteenth-century British scientist*

As the end of the 1800s approached, homes and industries in both the United States and Canada were growing increasing hungry for electric power, and eyes turned inexorably toward the ever-energetic Niagara. In 1891 a New York bank announced an international competition challenging scientists, engineers, and inventers to devise a practical method for generating large amounts of usable electricity at Niagara. Monitoring

Frozen mist takes on fantastic shapes in a wintry view of Horseshoe Falls.

the contest was famed British physicist Lord William Thomson Kelvin, whose name, as any high school science student knows, is permanently attached to the absolute scale for measuring temperature.

Kelvin thought the competition a splendid exercise, for he was the sort of scientist who had far less regard for nature than he did for technology. He hoped to see every last ounce of the Niagara's water channeled into canals, tunnels, and turbines for the purpose of

generating electricity. It troubled him not in the least that this would dry up the falls and completely spoil one of North America's most inspiring natural wonders—and he said so.

Kelvin's enthusiasm for the project was widely shared. At least twenty companies from around the world submitted plans, but if they had high hopes at the outset, these were soon dashed. The competition languished without a winner. No one could solve the daunting technical problems involved in generating so much electricity and then shipping it over considerable distances for use in factories, businesses, homes, and public buildings. Even the great Thomas Edison, the world-renowned oracle of electricity, had no viable solution for this particular riddle.

Thomas Edison (above) invested heavily in direct-current electrical systems, while his nemesis and one-time employee Nikola Tesla (below) invented efficient alternating-current generators. Tesla's designs turned Niagara into one of the world's mightiest power dynamos. The Niagara casino fountain (opposite) is dedicated to Tesla.

Was it possible, then, that a highly eccentric young Croatian by the name of Nikola Tesla possessed the answer? In 1882 Tesla had gone to work for Continental Edison in Paris and then, two years later, joined Edison himself in his New Jersey laboratory where the lightbulb, phonograph, motion-picture camera, and many other breakthrough inventions were born. This might have seemed the perfect place for a man with a restless and powerful mind like Tesla's. He read voraciously, had a photographic memory, had learned the logarithmic tables by heart, and could speak eight languages, including English, without an accent. When he was working on an invention, he did so without blueprints, drawings, or notes of any kind. But as it turned out, the laboratory was not large enough to contain two geniuses and two egos the size of those possessed by Edison and Tesla. Perhaps there was no building anywhere that large.

For one thing, Tesla was indeed eccentric; working with him must have been very difficult. It is said he was repulsed almost to the point of nausea by the sight of a woman wearing earrings. He believed that if he came near a peach, he would develop a raging fever. He claimed that his hearing was so sensitive that he could hear a watch ticking three rooms away. He told people that he personally communicated with extraterrestrials.

Tesla's boss, Thomas Edison, was brusque, stubborn, jealous of Tesla's accomplishments,

and, some would say, deeply suspicious of his assistants. The more brilliance they demonstrated, the less he was likely to tolerate them. Edison and Tesla did not get along—at all—and Tesla finally quit.

Out of work and embarrassed for funds, Tesla was temporarily reduced to doing manual labor. For a time he helped dig sewers in New York for as little as $2.00 a day, but a talent such as his would not long go unrecognized. George Westinghouse, another great inventor and a competitor of Edison's, lifted Tesla from the sewers with an offer so handsome that it effectively made him a rich man. Tesla received $60,000 for various patents plus royalties and a fat consulting contract in exchange for something Westinghouse wanted desperately: alternating current.

Tesla's link to Niagara Falls was forged long before the Croatian ever set foot in the United States. As a teenager he had seen pictures of the falls, and even then he had begun to dream of how all that fast-flowing water might be put to use. Simultaneously, he was fascinated by motion of a very different sort—electric currents.

By the time he went to work for Edison, Tesla had already devised a system for producing a new way to move and make use of electricity. Old-fashioned direct current moved electricity in only one direction, from the generator to an appliance such as a lightbulb. Tesla believed the current could be moved much more efficiently if it shifted back and forth in a cyclical manner, and he devised a way to do it. This breakthrough placed at risk the massive investments Edison had made in direct-current technology—and no doubt it contributed to the hard feelings that existing between the two inventors.

"Tesla believed that alternating current would make it possible to move large amounts of electricity over great distances," says historian Tom Yots. "Edison, on the other hand, wanted to stick with the older technology, which he felt was time-tested and reliable. Soon they were fighting back and forth over this."

Edison reacted to Tesla's ideas as if he had been personally affronted. He launched a public relations campaign extolling direct current and warning the public to avoid alternating current. To emphasize just how dangerous the new alternating current could be, he invited reporters to his lab to witness the electrocution of dogs and cats.

Tesla ignored Edison's jabs and by 1893 had pulled off his own public relations coup by lighting the enormous Columbian Exposition in Chicago with alternating current. No less a showman than Edison, Tesla made an appearance at the fair, during which he turned his own body into an electrical exhibit by allowing himself to receive a jolt of 200,000 volts, enough to cause his white tie and tails to radiate colorful halos of light. Tesla's audience went wild.

Building on these successes, Tesla focused his attentions on Niagara. Going on the lecture circuit, he claimed that if harnessed to alternating-current generators, Niagara Falls had enough energy to power every lightbulb and electric engine in the United States. Not only that, but it could heat homes and drive the machinery of entire industries. Tesla himself would

design the giant turbines and dynamos to make this possible. Now all that remained was to somehow tame that great big waterfall.

In fact, by the mid-1880s the process of domestication was already well under way. The key to tapping the vast power potential of the Niagara turned out to be not a canal but a tunnel. An entity at first called the Niagara River Hydraulic Power & Manufacturing Company and later known by the less chatty moniker of Niagara Falls Power had begun boring a tunnel through solid rock. Intended to drain off as much as possible of the river's energy-charged water and somehow put it to use, the Niagara Tunnel was no timid undertaking. Almost a mile and a half long, the tunnel was 21 feet high, 18 feet wide, and lined with several layers of brick. At least twenty-eight workers died during its construction, an effort that required the removal of 300,000 tons of rock while consuming twenty million bricks and 2.5 million board feet of lumber.

Tunnels carry much of the water used in Niagara hydroelectric plants. The tunnel above, however, is one of several scenic passageways chiseled through the solid rock to take visitors behind the falls.

There were those in Niagara Falls and elsewhere who wondered if this supertunnel might very well capture all the Niagara's water. Would it indeed dry up the falls? Local businessmen were understandably concerned that the tourists on which many of them depended might not be so readily attracted to a bone-dry, 180-foot cliff as to a mighty waterfall. These worries did not prevent them, however, from promoting the tunnel itself as a tourist attraction. Their advertisements and brochures described it as "the bore that is not boring."

Meanwhile, Niagara Power investors had worries of their own—even if the tunnel was not boring, it might nonetheless be financially ruinous to them. Their fears appeared well founded. Even as work on the tunnel proceeded, no one was entirely sure what would be done with the thing once it was completed. Large water turbines could be built and installed,

The Buffalo Railway's electric-powered Cold Spring Train ran between Main Street and the county poorhouse. After Niagara's huge turbines and alternating-current generators went online in the 1890s, trains like this one were in effect water powered.

but what machinery would they run? Electric generators made sense, but with existing direct-current technology, transmission lines could carry the current only about 2 miles, not even far enough to reach the nearby city of Buffalo.

Into this conceptual vacuum stepped Nikola Tesla with his grand notions. Tesla personally designed massive dynamos—each one weighing twenty-nine tons—to feed off the enormous volume of water rushing through the tunnel. He was sure these Goliaths would do the job. Success, he said, "was as firmly established as the air itself."

So few people shared his opinion that on the night work on the project was completed in 1895, the final switch linking the alternating-current generating system to Buffalo's electric power grid was pulled without fanfare or ceremony—after midnight! To nearly everyone's amazement—though not Tesla's—the very next morning Buffalo's streetcars were running on electricity produced at Niagara Falls.

"Harnessing the Niagara had been like calling on the genie in Aladdin's lamp," says Patrick McGreevy. "People felt the genie had a sort of limitless magical power. It could accomplish whatever you asked it to do, and you could ask it to do anything."

Tesla may or may not have looked upon the new Niagara powerhouse as Aladdin's lamp or himself as a genie, but when he visited the area in 1896, he pronounced the structure and its 5,000-horsepower dynamos to be "wonderful beyond comparison." Ironically, Tesla could not bear to stand near the big machines. Just as the sight of jewelry on a woman did, they made him feel sick. He left quickly, announcing that "the problem has been solved."

Scars that Never Heal

The Creator always gives and has always provided everything that we need.

—Jolene Rickard, Tuscarora Tribe

Those who stood beside Tesla in 1896 and watched him grow ill in the presence of the huge dynamos that he himself had designed may have thought that, despite the queasiness of it all, man had at last conquered nature. Of course that was not true, and sixty years later Niagara would make this clear in a thunderous and deadly way.

About five o'clock in the afternoon on June 7, 1956, strollers in Ontario's Queen Victoria Park were alarmed by a loud rumble on the far side of the river. The cliffs above Niagara's Schoellkopf (named for the man who had built Niagara's first hydroelectric plant) Power Station were suddenly in motion. They seemed to heave upward at first and then quickly began to disintegrate before the horrified eyes of observers. A rocky promontory 400 feet across and 40 feet thick crashed down onto the old plant, splitting the building wide open. Windows shattered and the roof collapsed, falling on the people and machinery inside. One worker was tossed out like a rag, and he tumbled down toward the river and to his death. Miraculously, thirty-eight others managed to claw their way to safety.

They got out just in time. The river—its tremendous forces pent up for decades in canals, tunnels, pipes, and turbines—was at last about to have its way with the plant. Mighty jets of water struck the generators, blowing them apart as if they were made of cardboard. Steel rods were bent and twisted like spaghetti, while ton-sized masses of brick and concrete crumbled and vanished into the torrent below.

To some observers it seemed as if a flight of unseen enemy warplanes had made a bombing run on the power plant—a highly successful one. Two-thirds of the plant had been destroyed, and the remainder was permanently off-line. In little more than a minute, a significant portion of the electric power production capacity in the northeastern United States had been snuffed out.

Even before this disaster, New York governor Thomas Dewey, who had unsuccessfully run for president twice and served three terms as the state's chief executive, had called for construction of a new, more modern and powerful plant. In fact, he demanded it. In 1954, as he approached the end of his last term as governor, Dewey had put in charge of the project Robert Moses, a man who knew how to get things done.

Moses was, in a way, an odd choice. Said one engineer who knew him well, "Bob Moses didn't know the first thing about electricity. If he licked his finger, stuck it in a socket, and it sparked, the circuit was alive. That was all he knew."

Even so, Dewey was sure he could rely on Moses, who typically responded to difficult assignments as if he were his biblical namesake. He always came down from the mountain with fire in his eyes and a single-minded determination. Arrogant and dictatorial, he had driven state workers and contractors to the breaking point to complete dozens of expressways and bridges, scores of public housing developments, and hundreds of parks and playgrounds. Many of these projects he brought in under budget and ahead of schedule, accomplishments made possible by Moses's unwillingness to let political opposition, sluggish contractors, farms, or houses stand in his way. He simply bulldozed them aside.

At Niagara, however, Moses met with resistance of a completely unfamiliar variety. His Niagara opponents possessed a will and patience such as he had never before encountered. They were Native Americans.

Moving ahead with the power plant project required construction of a sizable reservoir. It would store the water needed to put a little extra spin in the big power station turbines during peak hours, when homes and industries were consuming a lot of electricity. Unfortunately, the most likely site for such a reservoir was a 10-square-mile reservation belonging to a tribe known as the Tuscarora.

Centuries ago, before Europeans ever set foot in North America, the Tuscaroras lived in what is now North Carolina. Eventually they migrated north, where they allied themselves with the powerful Iroquoian League of Five Nations. The Iroquois gave the Tuscaroras a modest homeland near the Niagara River, where they remained for hundreds of years, farming and occasionally working in white-owned factories, but generally keeping to themselves.

There were still about 600 Tuscaroras on the reservation in 1956 when the Niagara cliffs fell on the Schoellkopf Plant, making the need for a new power station all the more urgent. State and power company officials soon approached the tribe with an offer to buy as much as half the reservation. The Tuscaroras had a quick answer for them—a very simple one. They said "no."

Moses was outraged and warned the Tuscaroras that if they did not sell, and sell quickly, he would have their land condemned to make way for the reservoir. Given Moses's reputation, this was no idle threat. He had successfully employed this tactic many times in the past, and as subsequent events would prove, he was more than ready to use it again.

Even so, the Tuscaroras refused to budge. Elton Greene, a respected tribal leader, explained the matter for the press. "We think our land is sacred," he said. "Money evaporates, but the land does not."

The contrast between Elton Greene and Robert Moses was stark. Moses was a stern, stiff-lipped elitist; Greene would laugh and gab with anybody. Moses had spent a lifetime wielding political power, as often as not for the benefit of the rich and well connected; Greene had taken life more or less as it came. Greene had been a farmer, a carpenter, a preacher, even a vaudeville performer. Now he was head chief of the Tuscaroras.

Niagara's Schoellkopf Power Station before and after a mighty rockfall devastated the complex in 1956.

"Robert Moses had in his mind that he was going to take this land regardless of treaties or anything else," says Eli Rickard, whose father, Clinton Rickard, a Tuscarora farmer and former chief, stood shoulder to shoulder with Greene during the tribe's confrontation with Moses. "This was what provoked our people. We tried to tell them there was no dollar value you could place on Indian land. We felt the land was priceless."

Undeterred, Moses offered more money. The tribe responded by ringing the reservation with NO TRESPASSING signs. For two years Moses kept raising the ante, and the Tuscaroras kept turning him away. "The braves are whooping it up," Moses said in disgust.

By 1958 Moses had had enough. In April he sent a large party of legal experts, workmen, and surveyors to the reservation line. Escorting them were thirty-five deputy sheriffs and fifty state troopers armed with teargas grenades and submachine guns and outfitted in full riot gear. The Tuscaroras were waiting for them.

"Robert Moses got impatient and brought in the surveyors, the dozers, and the police," says Rickard. "But we had heard they were coming." A tense standoff ensued as approximately 200 Tuscaroras placed themselves directly in the path of the workers and their police escorts. Many of the Tuscaroras on hand that day were women and children.

"An elderly lady and one of her grandchildren lay down in front of a bulldozer," says Rickard. "She said, 'Go ahead and spill my blood on this land, because I'm not going to let you in here.' And of course the operator wouldn't do that."

Recognizing that the use of raw force had its limits, Moses backed off, but only temporarily. Now he turned to the courts, where the Tuscarora tribe could not hope to match the savvy of the state's high-powered attorneys. By May the legal system had succeeded where bulldozers and riot police could not, and workers were finally clearing trees and brush to make way for the reservoir.

Meanwhile the legal battle continued all the way to the United States Supreme Court, where on March 7, 1960, the justices issued their final ruling: The state could take the Tuscarora land. Within a year, New York's new governor, Nelson Rockefeller, threw a switch putting online the new hydroelectric power station—named after Robert Moses—and what was at the time the largest hydroelectric complex in the world. Robert Moses had won.

"The power authority got its reservoir," Rickard says. "And we were left with scars that will never heal."

As it turned out, Niagara Falls, the ancient, watery natural wonder, would be scarred as well.

Cataract of Electricity:
Niagara Power Generation

More than 4.6 million kilowatts of electricity are generated from seven hydroelectric power plants on the Niagara River.

In the United States:

◆ Robert Moses Generating Station features thirteen generators producing 2.275 million kilowatts. Built as part of the Niagara Power Project funded by Congress and administered under the New York Power Authority, this enormous plant located several miles downriver from the falls opened in 1961.

◆ Lewiston Pump Generating Station and Reservoir includes twelve reversible pump-generators. During periods of low kilowatt usage, the plant stores water in a reservoir. When usage is high, the water flows down through the generators, producing 300,000 kilowatts.

In Canada:

◆ Sir Adam Beck No. 1 Generating Station, near Queenston, was completed in 1922. Its ten generators produce 470,000 kilowatts.

◆ Sir Adam Beck No. 2 Generating Station, located just south of the No. 1 plant, started generating power in 1954. Its sixteen generators produce 1.29 million kilowatts.

◆ Sir Adam Beck Pump Generating Station and Reservoir, completed in 1956, stores water heading for the falls at night and releases it during the day. Its six reversible generators produce 120,000 kilowatts.

◆ DeCew No. 1 Generating Station, located in St. Catharines, has five generators producing 23,000 kilowatts.

◆ DeCew No. 2 Generating Station, also in St. Catharines, has two generators producing 142,000 kilowatts.

◆ Fortis-Rankine Generating Station, completed in 1927 and located just 500 yards from the Horseshoe Falls, is off-line today. It is capable of producing 75,000 kilowatts in an emergency. Since the station's water rights end in 2009 and may not be renewed, it is unlikely that it will be returned to service.

The Robert Moses and Adam Beck stations sit opposite each other on the river. A tramway connects them, and their electrical power grids connect as well, making the combined generation the largest hydroelectric power producer in North America.

If They Turned Off the Falls

Sometimes the level of the water changes a little bit, but not much. If the hydroelectric people decide to change the level, they let us know. I can remember two or three times when they lowered the water significantly because there was somebody going over in a barrel or there was a boat caught up there.

—*Richard Schuyler, captain,* Maid of the Mist

During the 1890s, Lord Kelvin had envisioned a Niagara Falls with barely enough water dribbling over it to dampen a bath mat. That was, in fact, the way he wanted it. He preferred to see the falls' thundering waters put to work driving hydroelectric turbines. By 1960, when the Robert Moses Power Station began operation, Kelvin's vision became a real possibility.

As part of the water- and electric power-sharing agreement between the United States and Canada that helped make the new hydroelectric complex a reality, power stations on both sides of the border were allowed to use up to 75 percent of the Niagara River's flow. Both nations agreed that water should continue to flow over the brink of the two waterfalls, but at a reduced rate.

When left to follow its natural course and not drained off into canals, tunnels, and conduits, water rushes over the falls at an average rate of about 212,000 cubic feet per second. During daylight hours, when people are likely to be on hand to enjoy the spectacle of the falls, at least 100,000 cubic feet per second are allowed to pass through the upper rapids and over the precipice. The rest is captured and channeled into the turbines. At night and during winter, the falls' share is only 50,000 cubic feet; the other 75 percent is used to generate electricity.

"This is the essential paradox of Niagara Falls," says Patrick McGreevy. "We want the power, but we also want the falls. In the 1950s, when the treaty was worked out between the United States and Canada, people thought they had reached a compromise. But the compromise was between two nations, not between people and the river. The treaty basically said that two-thirds of the water will go through pipes and one-third will be left to pour over the falls."

Although it might be technically feasible to snatch all the Niagara's water and generate even more power, at present no one argues that should be done. The waterfall has tremendous commercial value as a tourist attraction. Given the increasing economic and political importance of energy, however, it is possible that the scenic, historic, and spiritual value of Niagara Falls may not be enough to save it. Even if the falls never again run dry—as has happened naturally on sev-

A yacht cruises past the walls of Fort Niagara and the massive structure sometimes referred to as the French Castle.

eral occasions—this greatest of North American wonders has been forever altered.

"We've diminished the falls," says Paul Gromosiak. "How can anyone say we haven't when we control the flow and we can turn the water on and off as if it were a faucet in a bathtub. You want to increase the flow? Turn a knob. You want to decrease it? Turn the knob the other way."

Without a doubt, human activity has greatly altered the appearance of Niagara Falls. During the 1850s, when Frederic Church painted his famous masterpiece with its blue-green waves pounding over the precipice, the water at the lip of the falls was more than 20 feet deep. Now it is little more than 5 feet deep. Having lost as much as 75 percent of its depth, much of that after the Robert Moses Power Station opened in 1960, the Niagara River no

Twentieth-century postcards celebrate the majesty of the falls, one of the world's first tourist destinations. Loss of the falls as an attraction would deal a severe blow to the Niagara-area economy. The famed Spanish Aero Car (opposite) has been carrying visitors over the swirling Whirlpool Basin for more than ninety years.

longer dropped in a great, white curtain around the Horseshoe. Instead most of the water fell where the river's current was strongest, near the center of the original waterfall. To restore or at least simulate the falls' historic appearance, engineers reworked the riverbed to distribute the water more evenly. This resulted in a waterfall that superficially resembled the one that Frederick Olmsted worked so hard to preserve, but it was no longer, strictly speaking, a product of nature.

"The falls didn't look so nice with more water going over the center than over the sides," says Gromosiak. "So during the 1950s we reshaped the bed of the river around the brink of the falls so that the water would spread out more evenly. That sort of thing has happened a lot in the history of the falls. It wasn't always the way we thought it should look. How do we think the Grand Canyon should look? Yosemite? Should we tamper with them, too, because they're not the way we think they should be?"

Still more hydroelectric power stations are scheduled to come online at Niagara during the next few years. It is said this will not change the "free-running" portion of the Niagara River and that the appearance of Niagara Falls will be left largely unchanged. However, with energy growing scarcer and more costly by the day, there are those who ask if the dry, dead waterfall envisioned by Lord Kelvin might yet become a sad reality.

Robert Moses:
New York's Parks and Power Czar

Among the most important New York power brokers of the twentieth century, the name of Robert Moses is often mentioned in the same sentence with the likes of Franklin D. Roosevelt, Alfred Smith, Jimmy Walker, Fiorello LaGuardia, and Thomas Dewey. In fact, his influence was so pervasive that the New York of today is in no small part a product of Moses's vision of the modern urban state.

Moses was not a politician in the usual sense and never held any high elective office. Instead he wielded the political power won by others, using it to establish parks and build roads, tunnels, and bridges. The Long Island Expressway owes its existence to his determination and political acumen, as does the United Nations complex and Lincoln Center in New York City and the Robert Moses Parkway and Robert Moses Power Station in Niagara Falls.

President Richard Nixon, Robert Moses, and Prime Minister Pierre Trudeau meet at a New York Power Authority anniversary event.

Born into a prosperous family in 1888, Moses studied political science at Yale and earned a Ph.D. at Columbia University in 1914. During the 1920s, New York governor Alfred Smith hired Moses as a speechwriter and brought him to Albany, where he became involved in an effort to establish a statewide park system. In 1933 Moses became director of the New York City Department of Parks, a job he held for nearly thirty years. Under his leadership the department increased the number of city parks nearly fourfold, to 777 in 1960. Over the years Moses also headed numerous other boards and committees overseeing key construction projects, many of them mammoth affairs, such as the Triborough Bridge and Tunnel.

When pursuing a new project or goal, Moses allowed nothing to stand in his way, and he used engineering reports, bulldozers, the courts, and even state troopers to enforce his will. Since many of the highways, bridges, and parks he controlled charged fees or tolls and also received state, municipal, and federal funds, Moses had enormous financial resources at his disposal. On occasion he applied these funds in ways that others considered high-handed or insensitive. His highway projects often slashed through neighborhoods and private property without regard to the consequences.

Although Moses had no degree or expertise in engineering or electric power production, he served as chairman of the power authority of the State of New York during the 1950s. Moses used the position to push for the redevelopment of New York's Niagara River frontage and to enhance the capacity of hydroelectric plants near Niagara Falls. This brought about his now-famous confrontation with the Tuscarora Nation over use of reservation property for a reservoir. Moses won the battle in the courts, but perhaps at a high cost to his personal power and esteem. By 1961, when the massive state-owned Robert Moses Power Plant went online, his political influence had begun to wane.

Romancing the *Falls*

Wide Awake in a Land of Dreams

One of my favorite places at night is right smack in the middle of the American Falls and the Canadian Falls. When the lights go on, and the falls are all lit up, it's . . . well, it's just illuminating.

—*Helena Harrington, owner of Two Lions B&B in Niagara Falls, Ontario*

"I never get tired of coming down here and putting on the lights," says Peter Gordon, who operates the powerful lights that give the American and Horseshoe Falls a wonderland appearance at night. "I always get a kick out it, especially during the summer when we've got maybe 35,000 people down there. It gives you a feeling of power, I guess."

Each evening from about 9:00 until midnight—the show starts earlier during the cold-weather months when the days are shorter—the Horseshoe and American Falls are converted into gigantic motion picture screens. Only, in this case, the screens are the movie—it's all about falling water, clouds of mist, and light. Sometimes the water is fired with colored light, making the falls look like an unusually bright display of the aurora borealis.

Visitors gather in the tens of thousands to witness these stupendous displays. In fact, many make the trip to Niagara just to see the falls lit up at night.

It is not entirely certain who came up with the idea of shining lights on Niagara Falls after dark, but the notion has been around since at least 1860, when the Prince of Wales came here to enjoy the world's best-known natural wonder. The prince met famous daredevil acrobat Blondin and was treated to an unusually thrilling rope-dancing display out over the Niagara Gorge. However, after a stay of several days, the man who would become King Edward VII upon the death of his mother, the nearly immortal Queen Victoria, went away with the impression that Niagara's best act was the waterfall itself. No doubt contributing to this feeling was a spectacular light show put on in his honor.

Produced by powerful spotlights passing through a kaleidoscope of colored gel, the colors that adorn the falls at night are constantly changing.

To light the falls and delight the prince, locals placed 200 Bengal lights behind both curtains of water. Often used in fireworks displays or by the military to illuminate battlefields at night, these long-burning flares cast a ghostly blue light on both the American and Horseshoe Falls. The effect was said to have been dazzling, much like that of a bright light passing through fine crystal.

Nearly twenty years would pass before the falls once more glowed at night. This time the illuminant was not a type of fireworks but rather electric-arc lamps of the type invented by Charles Brush. In 1879 the Brush Electric Company of Cleveland was engaged to illuminate the falls in honor of a visit by the Marquis of Lorne and his wife, Princess Louise. Brush placed twelve large lamps across from Horseshoe Falls and another four in front of American Falls. Power for the lamps was drawn from a waterwheel located in the rapids above the falls.

"The very first use of electric power at Niagara Falls was to shine a light on the falls—to do something unnatural to this natural wonder," says Patrick McGreevy. "Of course today we now have enormous numbers of lights shining on the falls every night."

The Brush lights remained in place for only one season, but as technology improved and electric power became more readily available, it was, perhaps, inevitable that the falls would be lit on a regular basis. The light shows were, after all, both spectacular and popular. During the 1890s the Maid of the Mist Boat Company began to brighten the falls at night with searchlights. In 1901, during Buffalo's Pan-American Exposition, an event that was itself aglow with countless thousands of electric lights, the falls were illuminated with searchlights.

By 1907 a more comprehensive system had been designed to light the falls. Consisting of thirty-six sizable electric lamps producing more than a billion candlepower, they were thousands of times brighter than the sixteen Brush arc lights that had lit up the falls three decades earlier. Surprisingly, all this light was directed only at the Americans Falls, which must have been bright enough to sting the eyes of observers. Workers were paid 50 cents a night to place tinted film in front of the lamps and paint the falls in all the colors of the rainbow.

Early attempts at evening illumination of the falls proved such a hit with tourists that eventually local businesses resolved to make the practice permanent. Except for interruptions of several years during each of the world wars and brief blackouts due to power station break-downs, the falls have been lit continuously now for more than a century.

During the 1920s U.S. and Canadian business leaders formed a group to make sure there was always enough money and lighting equipment available for the show to go on without undue interruption. At first known informally as the "Generators," the group soon evolved into a formal entity known as the Niagara Falls Illumination Board. Consisting of government and power company officials as well as businesspeople, the board still oversees funding and maintenance of lighting operations.

Niagara celebrates light and color almost as much as falling water. Each night powerful spotlights like those above turn the falls into spun-sugar rainbows (see opposite).

Gordon is one of two full-time staff operators employed by the board to oversee the nightly illumination. It takes only one of them to run the show from a small room overlooking the falls. Many visitors may mistakenly believe the colors they see appear at random or are selected by computer, but not so. Every few minutes, Gordon or his associate throws toggle switches to change the color of the various lights, and they rely on their own artistic sensibilities to produce the delightful kaleidoscope effect.

"It's great working with the colors," says Gordon. "I always get a kick out it."

Gordon says he starts with red and then mixes in blue, green, or yellow lights as the mood strikes him. He tries to make sure all the colors are not mixed in at once.

"In that case it goes totally black out there," he says.

Over the years, a variety of electric lamps have been used to light the falls. Among these were searchlights much like those used by the Royal Air Force to spot German bombers during the World War II Battle of Britain. The current system relies on high-voltage xenon arc lamps so powerful that they can create a rainbow over the falls.

It is easy to see why most visitors consider a trip to Niagara incomplete unless they have seen the falls at night. Said one mid-twentieth-century visitor: "Seeing the falls at night is to be wide awake in the land of dreams."

Wedding Journeys and Negative Ions

All that falling water has an influence on people's emotions. They call us the honeymoon capital of the world, so there are certainly a lot of people who see the romantic side of Niagara Falls.

—*John Williams, captain,* Maid of the Mist

What could be more romantic than a rainbow over Niagara Falls, especially one that can be seen and enjoyed at night? The lighting of Niagara Falls was only one of many miracles of technology associated with this extraordinary place, but the emotional impact it makes on people has little to do with science. We are all romantic beings at heart, and the falls speak most clearly and passionately to the part of us that responds to moonlight and the sound of moving waters. Just ask the countless thousands of couples who honeymoon beside the falls each year.

Before the middle of the nineteenth century, romantic-era poets and visionaries colored the way Niagara Falls was perceived. They saw the falls as emblematic of nature and the awesome power that underlies all existence. Even before the Civil War these attitudes had begun to give way to more scientific- and technology-oriented ideas and the notion that Niagara was a great, thundering mass of raw horsepower that could be corralled and put to work for human purposes. By the mid-twentieth century, however, people were once more thinking of the falls in romantic ways, only this time the romance was of a far more personal nature.

Instead of the raw forces of nature or a seemingly endless supply of electric current, the falls now exemplified the power of love. Seen as synonymous with youthful romance, Niagara became the world's first—and for a long time only—honeymoon resort.

No one knows for sure when Niagara began its long history as a honeymoon retreat. It is said that Vice President Aaron Burr's daughter Theodosia came here in 1801 to celebrate her approaching nuptials, although she was not yet married at the time. Some years later, Jerome Bonaparte, Napoleon's younger brother, appeared at the falls with his new and adoring wife at his arm. The Bonapartes' journey to the falls must have been very long and arduous, but countless other loving couples would later follow their example and, taking advantage of easier access, honeymoon beside the Niagara's roaring cataracts.

By 1859, when Blondin took his first walk across the Niagara Gorge on a tightrope, Niagara Falls had already become North America's favorite spot for what in those days was known as "the wedding journey." Because they were supposed to be, and no doubt often were, rapturous, these postnuptial excursions were sometimes humorously described as "honey lunacy." This gave rise to the term "honeymoon,"

People have been attracted to Niagara Falls since well before the invention of photography.

which we still use to describe a married couple's first trip together. Very often today, as in the past, the honeymoon will involve a trip to Niagara Falls.

Today Niagara Falls is heavily promoted as a honeymoon destination, but this was not always the case. Nor did it need to be. During the late nineteenth century, Niagara Falls honeymooners stepped down from railroad Pullmans in droves to be hurried to their hotels in horse-drawn hansoms. Novelist William Dean Howells wrote about one such couple in his 1888 novel, *Their Wedding Journey*. Therein, the young bride agonizes over the possibility that others may see her at Niagara Falls and know immediately that she has just gotten married. The last thing she wanted was to be an "evident bride." Even so, she looked very much forward to spending a few glorious days in a place where "the carking cares of business . . . fashion . . . age . . . sorrow . . . and heartbreak" were left behind to make way for the celebration of "youth, faith, and rapture."

"People have been coming to Niagara on their honeymoons for a long time," says Karen Dubinsky, author of *The Second Greatest Disappointment: Honeymooning and Tourism at Niagara Falls*. "Couples were coming here for at least a century before honeymooners became the tourist industry's lifeblood."

Niagara's reputation as a honeymooners' paradise reached its zenith during the years just after World War II. Flush with victory, U.S. and Canadian soldiers came home, bought a car, and did what young people have always done when they are not sure what to do next: They got married. Bumper-to-bumper highway jams of brand-new Fords and Chevys brought phenomenal numbers of newlyweds to the falls.

"Niagara Falls had an advantage over many other places as a honeymoon destination," says Dubinsky. "It was accessible by automobile to maybe 70 percent of North America's industrial working class. Most could get in their cars and be here in less than a day."

Yes, honeymooners could drive to Niagara Falls. U.S. Highway 62 would get them there. So would New York Highway 31, Ontario Highway 20, and perhaps a dozen other well-maintained arteries. But why did they come?

"I think they came because they had an image of Niagara Falls as a sexual place, a place of forbidden pleasures, titillating and dangerous," says Dubinsky. "It seemed a fitting place because the honeymoon represents one's entry into sexual culture. Coming to Niagara Falls for your honeymoon was a very public, shorthand way of announcing that you were now a sexual being."

Of course there was more to the attraction of Niagara Falls than a sexy reputation—the sheer majesty of the scenery, for instance. It is nearly impossible to look upon an impressive and beautiful scene without it stirring powerful emotions. And as we all know, strong feelings, whether of awe or love, are akin. But some believe the falls themselves exude an aura of primordial sexual energy. There are even those who think that around the falls, the air itself is sexy.

"That's the negative ion theory," says Dubinsky. "The idea is that the negative ions produced by all that falling water stir up certain feelings. Some people offer that as an explanation for the popularity of Niagara Falls as a honeymoon destination."

No doubt some people take the negative ion theory seriously. It is true that the moist air around falls sometimes seems to carry a slightly acerbic odor like the back of a television set or an electrical transformer. Possibly this is due to the grand array of power stations and transmission lines in the area, but more likely it is imaginary. Most Niagara Falls locals give a wink, a nod, and a chuckle when someone mentions the subject of negative ions.

THEIR MAJESTIES, KING GEORGE VI AND QUEEN ELIZABETH VIEWING NIAGARA FALLS FROM CANADIAN SIDE

Among the loving couples who have visited the falls were Britain's King George VI and his wife, Queen Elizabeth. Arriving in 1939 shortly before the outbreak of World War II, the royals dedicated the Rainbow Bridge, which would be completed the following year.

Ron Priefer, who teaches organic chemistry at Niagara University, is not sold on the negative ion theory. "If you look on the Internet, you'll find all sorts of interesting claims made about negative ions—for instance, that they'll clean the air and remove dust, smoke, pollen, and spores. They're also said to help you sleep, increase your physical and mental abilities, or decrease fatigue and depression. But is any of this true?"

Priefer doesn't necessarily think so. After all, negative ions are merely oxygen molecules that have picked up an extra electron. They can be created by cosmic rays, electromagnetic waves, the sun, lightning, and, yes, falling water. For obvious reasons, there may be an abundance of negative ions in the vicinity of Niagara Falls, but what difference does that make?

"Not much," says Priefer. "There's this myth that they serve as a powerful aphrodisiac, but that's not why people come here. They come because of the natural beauty. My wife and I love the falls, but I don't think that's because of negative ions."

The truth is, nobody knows for sure why people are attracted to one another, why they fall in love, or decide to get married. Nobody knows why nearly everyone loves waterfalls. They just do.

"What it comes down to is that Niagara Falls is a lot of water, a whole bunch of water falling over some rocks," says Dubinsky. "And that kind of makes you love it."

Norma Jean Takes a Walk

Let me tell you something. You're young, you're in love. Well let me give you a warning. Don't let it get out of hand like those falls out there.

—Joseph Cotten as George Loomis in Niagara *(Twentieth Century Fox, released 1953)*

By the 1950s—as scientists zeroed in on ways to control the atom, disease, the inner reaches of genetics, and the outer vastness of space—the physical world no longer seemed so far out of control. The only thing that was still uncontrollable, it seemed, was desire. In 1952, Desire herself came to Niagara.

She was born Norma Jean Mortenson, but the world will forever remember her by another, more melodic name—Marilyn Monroe. Raised a virtual orphan in a relatively poor section of Los Angeles, Norma Jean spent little time with her mother and never even knew the identity of her father. Like many young women in her circumstances, she married early. She was barely sixteen in June 1942 when she exchanged vows with her next-door neighbor, a rather ordinary man named Jim Daugherty.

It quickly became apparent, however, that Norma Jean, with her sparkling eyes and dyed, ever-so-blonde coiffure, was anything but ordinary. Having stumbled onto a modeling career, she quickly became the rage among the photographers who sold titillating pinups and the young soldiers who ogled them. By the late 1940s she had moved from barracks walls to the silver screen, but not as Norma Jean. Her producers believed she would be more marketable with a different name, and some studio genius—there are those who say it was Norma Jean herself—put together the rather musical combination of "Marilyn Monroe." It was a name impossible to pronounce without puckering one's lips.

Marilyn's early movies such as *The Asphalt Jungle*, *All About Eve*, *As Young as You Feel*, and *Monkey Business* made her a star. Most film historians agree, however, that Marilyn took her great leap into legend on a sunny day in June 1952, when she went for a walk along the cliffs beside Niagara Falls. Her walk, taken in a skin-tight black skirt and bright red blouse, was filmed from behind, every twitching inch of the way, by a camera rolling along a track.

Unlike so many other young, attractive women of the time, Marilyn had not come to the falls on a honeymoon. The overmatched Daugherty had been unceremoniously dispatched some years earlier in a California divorce court, and the actress was not yet ready to settle down. She had arrived a few days after her twenty-sixth birthday to film *Niagara*, a Twentieth Century Fox thriller starring Joseph Cotten as George Loomis, an intensely jealous husband, and Marilyn as Rose, his altogether unreliable wife. Unlike her previous movies, which had cast her mostly as a loveable trollop, this film required her to play not just a bad girl, but a very bad girl indeed.

Legendary screen star Marilyn Monroe became forever linked to Niagara Falls after she came here in 1952 to make the box-office blockbuster Niagara.

Rose and her scheming lover were set on disposing of the inconvenient Loomis—by dumping him into the falls, no less.

Hollywood could hardly have found a better setting for a story like this one, which relies less on plot than on an overarching atmosphere of peril, something Niagara Falls has been serving up to visitors for centuries. Some say the sense of danger that pervades this place, where the waters of a vast continental heartland drop over a sheer cliff, is central to its attraction. Certainly it adds to the romance of the falls since, as everyone knows, danger intensifies passion.

"Marilyn Monroe's portrayal of Rose in the movie *Niagara* is very sensuous," says author Patrick McGreevy. "Rose is a very sexy woman, and she is in Niagara Falls, which is depicted as a place of danger where one is likely to fall into sin of one sort or another. This

Niagara-on-the-Lake

Niagara-on-the-Lake occupies the former site of a Neutral (Onondaga) Indian village on Lake Ontario, just west of the Niagara River. Settled during the early 1780s by British loyalists migrating from Revolutionary-era New York and Pennsylvania, it consisted at first of only sixteen farm families who had resolved to start a new life on Canadian soil. The community prospered, but the town that grew up in the protective shadow of Fort George was almost totally destroyed by invading U.S. forces during the War of 1812. Rebuilt soon after the war, the old town remains today one of the most historic in Ontario or all of Canada.

Visitors are attracted to Niagara-on-the-Lake by its quaint appearance, lovely lakeside scenery, numerous historic and cultural attractions, and, of course, its proximity to Niagara Falls. Relaxing inns and B&Bs abound, as do enticing restaurants. Fort George, with its pentagonal stone walls, is only one of many historic sites. Among the best-known local events is the annual Shaw Festival. Held from July to early October, it features the plays of razor-witted Irish playwright George Bernard Shaw and other dramatic productions. Old Town offers some of the most delightful shopping experiences in the Niagara area. To plan a visit, contact the Niagara-on-the-Lake Chamber of Commerce and Visitors Bureau at (905) 468–1950, or visit www.niagaraonthelake.com.

image of the falls has a long history. People have often said the falls release a passion, a force of nature within us that we can't control."

Indeed, there was danger lurking at Niagara Falls, not just for the fictional George and Rose Loomis but also for the real-life Marilyn Monroe. She was about to be caught in a deluge of success that would end up drowning her. Her portrayal of Rose and her sultry walk at Niagara's Table Rock would prove the cultural equivalent of the Great Falls themselves. Six months after she left Niagara Falls, Marilyn appeared, sans red blouse and black skirt, in the very first issue of *Playboy* magazine, and a torrent of sensuality was unleashed upon a previously stuffy America.

Marilyn went on to star in eleven more major movies, including box-office block-busters such as *Gentlemen Prefer Blondes*, *How to Marry a Millionaire*, *River of No Return*, and *Bus Stop*. In 1954, a year after the release of *Niagara*, she married famed baseball slugger Joe DiMaggio, known to his millions of fans as the "Yankee Clipper." DiMaggio had been dating the actress for about two years, and it is said he traveled to Niagara Falls to be near her during filming of the movie's location sequences. Unfortunately, this marriage proved even shorter than Marilyn's first. It lasted only about nine months, ending in October 1954 because of what the couple cited as "career conflicts."

Later Marilyn would enjoy a longer stretch of matrimony with noted playwright Arthur Miller, author of classic works such as *Death of a Salesman* and *The Crucible*, a play about the Salem Witch Trials, which he intended as a critique of McCarthyism. In 1956 Miller himself was bewitched—by Marilyn Monroe—and they were married in June. The marriage lasted nearly five years, ending in divorce in early 1961. Nineteen months later, Marilyn died in her Brentwood, California, home from an apparent overdose of sleeping pills. She was only thirty-six years old. Some say she had never recovered from her breakup with Miller. Others say she was a victim of her own wildly popular public image. Still familiar to fans everywhere—some of them born long after Marilyn's death—it was an image that will forever be linked to Niagara Falls.

"I think we can credit Marilyn Monroe with helping to reinvent Niagara Falls," says Dubinsky. "The filming of *Niagara* in 1952 was a huge event and was itself a big tourist attraction. There was lots of publicity, and during the summer of 1953, after the movie was released, more than thirteen million people visited the falls. The hotels were packed. The motels were packed. There were so many tourists that the chamber of commerce was issuing regular bulletins asking local citizens to please open up their houses to visitors."

Although Marilyn Monroe never actually honeymooned in Niagara Falls, the film *Niagara* proved something of a honeymoon for the actress and millions of adoring fans. It was something they would never forget. No doubt thousands of newlyweds have thought of her when they traveled to the falls to learn about love, passion, and the dangers that inevitably accompany them.

Two Hearts and Two Waterfalls

People say there must be some special sexual energy here. I don't know. I once heard it said that there really wasn't anything else to do when you came here, but I'm not so sure that's the answer either. I just think there's a wonderful feeling about yourself when you're here. And that in itself is a form of sexual energy.

—*Tom Yots, Niagara Falls historian*

People don't just honeymoon at Niagara Falls; lots of them get married here, too. Reverend Karen Hansen knows—she has performed more than 800 of the ceremonies herself. She runs the Two Hearts Wedding Chapel in Niagara Falls, Ontario, which is housed in a former Kentucky Fried Chicken restaurant.

"Niagara Falls is still the honeymoon capital of the world," says Hansen. "A lot of people get married here and then honeymoon by the falls because that's what their grandma and grandpa did; they want to carry on the family tradition. Others want to start a new tradition of their own."

However, some of the marriage ceremonies Hansen performs seem to have very little to do with tradition. "We had one wedding this past Halloween, with the bride and brides-maids all dressed as angels and the groom and groomsmen all dressed as devils," she says. "It was a beautiful wedding."

The sports world occasionally gets into the act as well. "A few years ago I performed a hockey team wedding," says Hansen. "The bride and groom were on opposing hockey teams, so they came in their hockey uniforms and asked me to wear a referee's shirt. Their wedding cake was an ice rink with a little puck and little players."

Not all of Hansen's weddings are performed at the chapel. "We get them married in hotel rooms, helicopters, and airplanes," she says. "I've even done weddings on Jet Skis. I'll do anything to make them happy except bungee cord jumping. I won't do a wedding on bungee cords."

A Jet Ski or bungee cord wedding might be overly rigorous for some of Hansen's less youthful couples. "We have more than a few older couples getting married," says Hansen. "We had a gentleman and his bride in here last October. He was eighty-five, and she was eighty-four, and it was the first wedding for both of them. They came all the way from Florida to Niagara Falls because they wanted to do it right when they got married. It was great. They got married and then went off to do the usual things. They went to the butterfly conservatory. They went on *Maid of the Mist.*"

The *Maid of the Mist* tour boats are themselves a popular location for weddings, and Hansen has married any number of couples onboard. After all, what setting for nuptials could be more dramatic than a great 180-degree curtain of water reaching toward the sky? However, most couples prefer to stand on dry land to take their vows—even if, in this case, dry is more a figure of speech than fact.

"The younger couples like to get married right beside the falls," says Hansen "It gets pretty damp out there sometimes. The old couples usually aren't too crazy about getting wet, but the young ones don't seem to care. They'll get married in a blizzard if they can do it down by the falls and have their pictures taken with Niagara Falls in the background."

On almost any day during warm weather months, photographers can be seen lining up brides, grooms, and their families and friends for wedding pictures beside the falls. But, of course, not all of the weddings here are large family affairs.

Reverend Karen Hansen has performed more than 800 Niagara wedding ceremonies—some of them in helicopters and airplanes and even on Jet Skis. However, most couples want to tie the knot down by the falls.

"We have plenty of elopements," says Hansen. "Some people just want to sneak away and spend a weekend in Niagara Falls without the family. They get married and then carry on with their lives."

Did Hansen herself get married and honeymoon in Niagara? "Well, no, believe it or not," she says. "We went to the Dominican Republic, mostly because I'd never been there. But I know plenty of residents of Niagara Falls who come down here, get married, and rent a hotel room for a couple of days. It gets them away from their apartments even though they're still in Niagara Falls. It's a new scene for them, and when you're getting married, that's nice."

Or maybe, like so many other couples who come here from elsewhere, they just love the falls. "It's absolutely beautiful here," says Hansen. "I love it at night, in winter, anytime. And if anybody wants to see the falls, that's great. I'm always happy to show them."

Alone in a Niagara Falls Crowd

People need a reflective space where they can go to think about what this life is all about. Niagara Falls provides that kind of experience if one is open to it.

—*Jolene Rickard, Tuscarora Tribe*

"Musicians are often alone, especially when they're on the road," says well-known song-writer, guitarist, and recording artist Artie Traum. "To be alone in a busy, touristy, romantic place like Niagara Falls is a very alienating experience."

It is an experience, a feeling, Traum has often had in the past, and not just at Niagara Falls. Traum has been writing and performing soulful vocal and acoustic guitar music since the 1960s, and he has stood on the same stage with James Taylor, Kris Kristofferson, Joni Mitchell, Debbie Andersen, Eric Kaz, and many other stars of the American popular music scene. But even when one's a star it is possible to get lonely, so Traum decided to write a song about it—a song called "Niagara."

"It's about getting stuck in Niagara Falls without your partner of choice," says Traum, "without somebody you care about."

> Well-known folk and jazz musician Artie Traum is one of many artists inspired by North America's best-known natural wonder. His soulful song "Niagara" deals with the irony of being alone in a place like Niagara Falls, with its crowds of tourists.

A native of the Bronx, Traum started out as a folk musician playing in Greenwich Village and at the Newport Folk Festival. During the 1970s he earned an international following as an acoustic guitarist, performing on stages in Europe, Japan, and the United States, where he appeared at Carnegie Hall and in countless other musical venues. Sometimes it was a lonely life.

"The inspiration for the song was coming to Niagara Falls and actually being alone there," says Traum. "When you're on the road and you're alone, there's this sense of longing, of missing somebody, and those feelings really seemed profound here at Niagara Falls."

As with Michael Daugherty (see the next chapter) and his symphonic band piece, however, Traum took part of his inspiration for "Niagara" from the falls themselves. "Musicians are inspired by Niagara Falls because of the powerful tone the falling water generates," says Traum. "The incredible sounds coming off the falls, the beautiful surroundings, the way the river flows—all those things really speak music to me as they do to other musicians."

Traum is one who thinks the negative ions stirred up by all that falling water may make a difference as well. "There are negative ions floating around, and that's something you feel viscerally," says Traum. "I can't tell you what a negative ion is. I'm a musician, not a chemist, but I mean it actually changes your mood to be here."

The mood of Traum's "Niagara" is distinctly blue. "There's this line in the song that just gives me goose bumps whenever I sing it. It goes, 'There's a wall of white water, but it only makes a body blue.' That really says everything that needs to be said about being alone in Niagara Falls."

At Last, Fortissimo

Watermusic

Falling water makes music, and I've never heard a symphony more beautiful than Niagara.

—Tourist at Table Rock in 1986

Father Louis Hennepin, who claimed to have been the first European to see—or hear—Niagara Falls, said the "roaring and bellowing of the water" was so "dreadful" that it might ruin a person's hearing. Most visitors today are delighted by the same scene that terrified the old French friar who carried around his own personal altar. To many the falls *are* an altar; there are even those who say they can hear the singing of angels in the rush of the rapids and the crash of the falls. In fact, lots of people hear music in falling water, but it does not always remind them of angels.

Among those able to detect the cadences of music in the roar of the falls is American composer Michael Daugherty, who apparently hears music everywhere and in everything. For decades he has been describing the North American landscape and culture in exquisite symphonic and chamber compositions with titles such as *Metropolis, Motorcity Triptych,* and—*Niagara Falls.*

"Music is a very abstract art form," says Daugherty, but he believes it can and should be accessible to ordinary people. "That's one of the reasons I use titles like 'Route 66,' 'Jackie O,' or 'Dead Elvis.' In fact, many of the pieces I've written have been inspired by American icons, and probably the greatest of those is Niagara Falls, the ultimate tourist trap."

Visitors at the brink of American Falls (left) in Niagara Falls State Park.

Because of the distinctly American flavor of his music, Daugherty has been compared with Aaron Copland, composer of *Rodeo, The Red Pony,* "Fanfare for the Common Man," and many other well-known symphonic classics. Perhaps best known of Copland's works is *Appalachian Spring,* a ballet score, which many believe was partly inspired by the tumbling brooks of the Appalachian Mountains. Actually, Copland said he had only one thing in mind when he wrote the piece: the artistry of the great American ballet performer Martha Graham—and that it was Graham herself who gave the piece its title. However, in the imagination of the public, the association of the piece with mountain streams and waterfalls grew so strong that Copland said even he began to see them when he conducted the ballet.

Unlike *Appalachian Spring,* Daugherty's *Niagara Falls* was indeed inspired by rushing water—quite a lot of it. "This particular river is no mountain spring," says Daugherty. "So whereas Copland's music can be very light and lilting at times, my music is rather Gothic. You have these different streams of water coming together and then this giant wall of sound."

Obviously the bigness of Daugherty's *Niagara Falls* is appropriate to its subject, and there *is* something alarming about it. A thundering band piece almost ten minutes long, it gives rise to feelings not unlike those described by Father Hennepin and by visitors today when they first lay eyes on the great falls. At times it's a little, maybe more than a little, awe-inspiring.

"All that water cascading over these huge rocks can be scary," says Daugherty. "If you stand near the brink of the falls and look down, it's terrifying; that terror inspired me to write some very dark moments into the music."

It's not all dark, of course. There's plenty of delight in the piece as well and lots of what some might call "descriptive passages."

"The piece starts out with a pounding rhythm, timpani playing *bom-bom-bom-bom-bom-bom-bom-bom-bom,*" says Daugherty. "It's pulsating and rhythmic, much like what you hear—what I hear—at the falls."

Repeated throughout are four powerful chords, which represent the words *Niagara Falls* as they are usually pronounced, not in five syllables but in four: *Ni-a-gra-Falls.* "You hear the chords *dee-da-dee-da,* and that's *Ni-a-gra-Falls,*" says Daugherty. "You can actually sing to it: *Ni-a-gra-Falls.*"

Accompanied by those four big chords, listeners take a symbolic journey to the falls, to the power plants in the gorge below, and to the tourist mecca above. There are daredevils riding over the falls in barrels. There are haunted houses and wax museums. And there is electricity pulsating through it all.

"When I wrote *Niagara Falls,* I couldn't help thinking about all that electricity coming out of the power plants," says Daugherty. "I couldn't help thinking about people doing crazy things like going over the falls in barrels. The falls stimulate people to do wild, crazy things. I think that's why so many people come here on their honeymoons."

Daugherty's own parents honeymooned here during the 1950s. Daugherty himself frequently visits the falls and still finds them stimulating and motivating. This is all the more understandable given the fact that his *Niagara Falls* band composition is so widely performed and has won him worldwide acclaim.

"People seem really excited about this piece," says Daugherty. "It resonates, perhaps the way the falls do. You have these two different things going. You have the sublime beauty of nature and at the same time all this bizarre American culture that has been drawn to it. I think my music does that, too. It's a very eclectic, strange sort of music that pulls together lots of different feelings and thoughts related to American life."

Naturally, Daugherty's piece ends with a big splash. "A very big splash," he says.

American Falls drops about 90 feet onto a jumble of rocks and boulders—unlike nearby Horseshoe Falls, which plunges about twice that distance, mostly into open water.

A Picture Worth Just One Word

The definition of skill is to walk a tightrope over Niagara Falls. The definition of intelligence is not to try.

—Adage of unknown origin

"Wow!" That's what people—kids especially—say when they see pictures of themselves riding over Niagara Falls like Annie Taylor did in 1901 or walking over the Niagara Gorge on a tightrope as if they were the Great Farini.

"We superimpose them against backdrops of the greatest attraction in the world," says Tom Terzakis, manager of the digital photo booths at Niagara Falls Park in Ontario. "That's Niagara Falls, and it's their imagination that makes the pictures come alive, right?"

Terzakis's customers don't actually have to jump into the rapids or poise on a wire at a dizzying height to get their pictures taken. All they have to do is pose for the camera, jump up and down, or do whatever they like. The lens and the digital electronics do the rest.

In the old days, before the advent of sophisticated digital technology, trick photographs were taken using crude, silent-movie-style sets. Subjects would stand in front of a false backdrop or behind it with only their heads or the upper part of their torsos showing. Tucked away in dusty old scrapbooks all over the United States and Canada are faded brown photographs featuring the head of somebody's great uncle or aunt superimposed on an unlikely body doing something even less likely—diving into Niagara Falls, for instance. People still enjoy having pictures like that made, but today it's all done with computers.

"We get a lot of families that just want their good side taken as they stand there and enjoy the beautiful scenery," says Terzakis. "But there are also those *fun* families who want to jump up and have us capture them in midair. Then we connect the photograph with an actual background that shows them being tossed over the falls. So you might have a dad wanting to get rid of the mum and pushing her over with an evil smile on his face and the kids in the background laughing."

Visitors often ask for photographs of themselves doing something impossible. "Our staff created a surfboard option that shows people surfing the rapids," says Terzakis. "That's pretty popular; so is the tightrope option that shows them walking over the falls on a rope."

It's all in good fun, of course, and no deception is intended. After all, who would imagine a photograph of a ten-year-old surfing Niagara Falls was the real thing. It's a souvenir, plain and simple, and a delightful one at that.

Computerized trick photography provides tourists with delightful souvenirs of their visit to Niagara Falls. Although far less technically sophisticated, old-fashioned studio shots like the vintage one opposite could produce extraordinary effects.

"The long version of our story is that we're a photo company," says Terzakis. "The short version is we make memories. We help thousands and thousands of people hold onto their memories and share them with others. It's an interesting business, and we see brand-new faces every day."

Trick photography and, indeed, photography itself probably have a longer history at Niagara Falls than at any other place in North America. In fact, the falls were a prominent and popular subject of some of the world's earliest commercial photographs. During the 1840s North American photographers adapted a French photographic technique known as daguerreotype and used it to make images of surprising quality for the times. Most such images were touched up or hand-colored by an artist. Employing this new technology, daguerreotypists such as Albert Southworth and Josiah Hawes made portraits of famous people, including Oliver Wendell Holmes, Henry Wadsworth Longfellow, Ralph Waldo Emerson, and former U.S. president John Quincy Adams. Many daguerreotypes featured natural subjects and, not surprisingly, the earth's most famous expanse of scenery—Niagara Falls. These early photographs of the falls were widely distributed and, in a fashion suggestive of Terzakis's computer manipulation of twenty-first-century photographic images, were frequently mounted in stereoscopic viewers that seemed to bring the roaring cataract to life.

Power of the Water

You get better rainbows toward the end of the day. That's also when you tend to get your socks wet. Aside from the wet feet, though, it's pretty cool no matter when you come.

—*John Williams, captain,* Maid of the Mist

It is estimated that twelve million people view Niagara Falls each year. That's about four times as many as visit Yellowstone National Park and more than a third the number of tourists attracted to the entire sin-and-sex city of Las Vegas annually. A metropolis with that many people would dwarf Los Angeles, Chicago, or even New York's own eight-million-strong Big Apple. And yet, it is probably safe to say that every single person who visits the falls takes from the experience something that is uniquely their own.

Many of Niagara's millions of tourists choose to stay in a motel or one of the big hotels or resorts that have sprung up on both sides of the border. However, more than a few prefer the quiet, friendly atmosphere of a bed-and-breakfast inn. Among the most popular of these is the Lion's Head B&B on River Road in Niagara Falls, Ontario. Located in a historic 1910 craftsman-style

Nowadays rainbows are not the only colorful attractions in Niagara. Below, a brightly lit glass forest rises over the entrance of the Seneca Niagara Casino in Niagara Falls, New York.

home once owned by Hugh Wilson, an early-twentieth-century president of the Toronto Power Company, it is loaded with old-fashioned elegance and charm. However, many guests think the best thing about the Lions Head is that it's only a ten-minute walk from the falls. This proximity is a special plus for first-time visitors, since it allows them to check in and then approach the falls just as the early explorers did—on foot.

Helena Harrington operates the Lion's Head, and over the years she has watched how her guests react to the falls. "They go out to the falls, out on the *Maid of the Mist*, over Rainbow Bridge, or down in the Cave of the Winds, and the power of the water has an unbelievable effect on them," says Harrington. "They take off their raincoats and they get soaked, of course, but there's also this sense of being completely drenched by the power of the falls. It has a spiritual effect on them."

Those who live and work near the falls are not immune to its influence. "It's like a living entity," says Harrington—and a noisy one at that. "You hear it all the time. When I first moved here I thought I was hearing a highway, but eventually I realized it was the roar

of the falls. I understand why the Native Americans called it Thundering Water. It's also easy to understand why people come here to see it. When I'm riding on the bike path or out walking, I look. I just have to look at all that white water pouring and pouring. It never stops, and I find that very humbling."

Like many others, Harrington believes the immense attraction of the falls may be due in part to negative ions generated by the churning water. "I always tell my guests that the falls are powerful enough to produce negative ions. I haven't really done much reading on it, but some people believe these negative ions can have an effect on the serotonin gland. This can make you feel good and positive, and it is also supposed to affect your sexuality. Maybe that's why they say we're the Happiness Capital of the World."

Not everyone who visits Niagara Falls finds happiness or passion here. Nor is everyone elated, awed, or inspired by Niagara's grand spectacle. In fact, some are downright unimpressed.

"Certainly when Father Louis Hennepin first saw the falls in 1678, he was awed," says historian Sherman Zavitz. "Most of the people who've come after him have also had strong feelings about the experience, but not everybody. Oscar Wilde, for example."

Widely known and celebrated for his outrageously funny plays, such as *The Importance of Being Ernest,* and equally outrageous lifestyle, Wilde visited the falls in 1882 and used the occasion to exercise his

Visitors attempt to take their Niagara experience with them in the form of photographs, but while pictures may be lost or fade with time, the emotional impact this mighty phenomenon makes on them will last forever.

famously acerbic wit. "The Niagara Falls," said Wilde, "is simply a vast amount of water going the wrong way over some unnecessary rocks. The sight of that waterfall must be one of the earliest and keenest disappointments in American married life."

A generation earlier, the falls had elicited an earthier dismissal from the no-nonsense British maid who accompanied Charles Dickens's wife, Kate, to Niagara in 1842. "It's nothing but water," said the maid. "And far too much of that."

For the great majority of those who have come here, and nearly all of Harrington's guests, however, seeing Niagara Falls is a passionate and highly positive experience, maybe even a life-changing one. "One of my recent guests who had just been on the *Maid of the Mist* told me that seeing the falls was a spiritual experience for her," says Harrington. "She said it was a cleansing experience like a baptism."

Does Harrington feel that way about Niagara Falls? "I understand the power of the water," she says. "But I don't understand why there is so much of it."

Waters of Life and Death

We picked up a young boy named Roger Woodward who was swept over the falls in 1960. Then a few years ago we had a really unbelievable rescue attempt when a guy came over the brink just in his street clothes. He popped right up in the Horseshoe, and the *Maid of the Mist* tried to reach him but couldn't because he was a little too close to the falls. Somehow he managed to flounder his way to shore, and they pulled him to safety.

—*John Williams, captain,* Maid of the Mist

During the 1970s author Patrick McGreevy worked the late shift at a factory in Niagara Falls, New York. One night, while on an extended break, he decided to take a long walk. There was no moon, and McGreevy's youthful legs quickly carried him beyond the glow of the city lights. Soon he could hear the thunder of falling water, and the sound drew him toward it just as it had Father Hennepin centuries earlier and just as it has so many others since. In the darkness ahead, he could see it, the black mass of the Niagara rolling down over the falls. He stood there transfixed by the spectacle until he heard someone call out from behind.

"Don't do it!" commanded a human voice. It was a policeman patrolling the area to guard against tragic accidents and equally tragic non-accidents. Having assured the officer that he had nothing in mind more dramatic than a bracing evening stroll, McGreevy was then curtly informed that Niagara Falls was "closed."

McGreevy relates this delightful if rather poignant anecdote in the preface to his book *Imagining Niagara* (University of Massachusetts Press, Amherst, 1994). By examining the widely varying visions and perceptions people have held of this extraordinary phenomenon over the centuries, McGreevy's book makes it clear that Niagara Falls is never really closed. While the parks may be chained and locked at night and half the Niagara's volume diverted into tunnels and piped into power plants, the river keeps pouring over the brink twenty-four hours a day, just as it has for thousands of years.

Perhaps more important, McGreevy points out, the falls continue to run full force in our hearts and minds. Niagara Falls has long been and remains to this day among the most potent of human symbols. Representing power and passion, life and death, it is emblematic of existence itself. It serves as a reminder, at the deepest levels of our consciousness, that life is always poised on a brink.

"Poets and other writers have often compared life to a river," says McGreevy. "They have described the Niagara as a river of life that flows from the past into the future. Now this is not the only river described that way, but the Niagara is unique in that it's a river with an abrupt break that separates the past from the future. As with life, the Niagara gets to a certain point and then drops off a cliff."

Since at least the nineteenth century, daredevils and stunters have dramatized this symbolic relationship by coming to Niagara Falls and physically placing themselves on the knife's edge between life and death.

A cable and breeches buoy are used to rescue Buffalo bargeman James Harris from a rock near the brink of Horseshoe Falls on August 7, 1918. Harris's barge had broken free and drifted down the Niagara River toward disaster.

A winter scene at Horseshoe Falls (above). The Niagara Falls Fire Department effects a rescue (opposite) near Chippawa Creek in August 1981.

Blondin and Farini did it by walking across Niagara Gorge on ropes and wires. Annie Edson Taylor and other stunters did it by riding over the falls in barrels and other all-too-flimsy contraptions—often with fatal results. It is easy to believe that anyone attempting stunts as dangerous as these must harbor a not altogether secret death wish.

"They wanted to challenge the power of the falls and, in doing so, to defy death," says McGreevy.

Others have come to Niagara, not to defy death but to embrace it. At least a thousand people are thought to have intentionally ended their lives with a dramatic plunge over the falls. Some have left notes containing last-minute goodbyes or instructions on how to dispose of their property. Others have left behind watches, automobiles, or even their clothes. Often the bodies of Niagara suicides are later found downstream, but many simply disappear and are never seen again.

It is true that not all feelings associated with Niagara Falls are happy ones. Victorians often said that Niagara, with its chaos of falling water, made them melancholy—or gave them terrible headaches. Visitors as far back as the seventeenth century and the time of the early explorers said they were overwhelmed with awe and the sense they were standing in the presence of great danger. Some even said they could feel the falls tugging at them as if drawing them into its deadly torrent.

"One of my guests had just come back from Table Rock," says B&B operator Helena

Harrington, "and he said, 'My goodness, Helena, I felt the falls calling me.'"

Of course, one does not have to be depressed or to have given up on life to hear that call. Many have reported hearing it or feeling the river's pull. Probably most of us who visit the falls do, although we may not be prepared to admit it.

"Harriet Beecher Stowe (author of *Uncle Tom's Cabin*) said she felt as if she could merge with the water and it would be a beautiful thing," says McGreevy. "Ralph Waldo Emerson (the nineteenth-century New England philosopher) said that when you look at nature, you're looking at a mirror—you're seeing yourself. You're seeing something that looks just like you staring back at you. It's true that many people have found themselves able to identify completely with Niagara Falls. We don't know if some of the people who jumped in did it because of these same sentiments, but we do know that over and over again people express these kinds of sentiments—that it would be a beautiful death."

Likely one reason visitors are prone to think about death is because Niagara Falls is, in fact, a dangerous place. A number of people have been swept over the falls who never had any intention of taking such a plunge. Their boat overturned or they got too close, slipped on a rock, and fell into the river.

Probably the most famous of these incidents took place on a July weekend in 1960, when a small aluminum boat got caught in the strong current above the falls. In the boat were James Honeycutt, age forty; teenager Deanne Woodward; and her seven-year-old brother, Roger. A friend of the Woodward family, Honeycutt was treating the youngsters to a Saturday afternoon of swimming. The excursion turned deadly after Honeycutt ventured beyond the so-called "point of no return" and lost control of his tiny vessel in the rapids. Honeycutt's desperate attempt to reach Goat Island failed when a large wave flipped over the boat, tossing out its hapless passengers and placing them at the mercy of the river's violence.

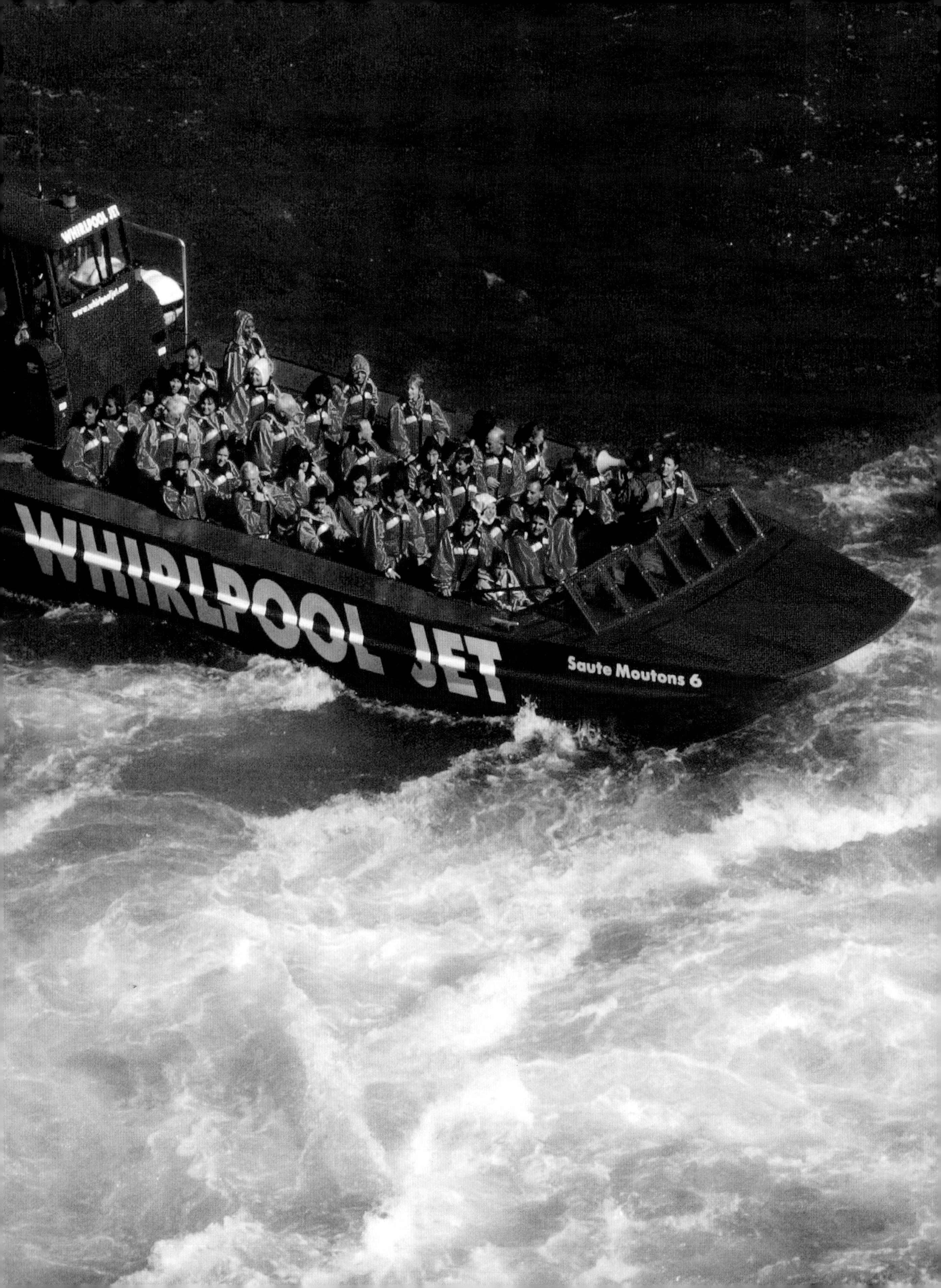
WHIRLPOOL JET
WHIRLPOOL JET
Saute Moutons 6

Struggling against the current, Deanne Woodward got within a few yards of Goat Island, where a pair of New Jersey tourists risked their lives to pull her safely ashore. Meanwhile, Honeycutt and the younger Woodward were swept past the island and over Horseshoe Falls. Unlike the children, Honeycutt was not wearing a life jacket; he would not be seen alive again. Roger Woodward, on the other hand, was about to become the central figure of a Niagara Falls legend.

Below the falls, *Maid of the Mist* captain Clifford Keech had no idea that anything unusual had happened above, so he was all the more astonished when Woodward's small form popped out of the roiling waters at the foot of the Horseshoe. Maneuvering the *Maid* with consummate skill, Keech got close enough to toss the boy a life preserver and pull him aboard. Astonishingly, the grade-schooler had sustained only a few minor cuts and abrasions. His survival has often been described as the "Miracle of Niagara Falls."

"Some people see Niagara Falls as a beautiful, life-giving fountain," says McGreevy. "Others see it as a terrifying wild beast."

It is, of course, both those things.

Niagara the Sublime

Although it was wonderful seeing all that water tumbling down, it would have been even more wonderful to see all that water tumbling up.

—*Mark Twain*

Honeymoons, anniversaries, weekend getaways, business meetings, conventions, nature outings, school excursions, family reunions, or simple curiosity—these are the sorts of reasons people typically give for visiting Niagara Falls. Likely, though, their motives are far more complex and run far deeper than they think. The falls are a natural and cultural phenomenon of enormous importance imbued with an almost mystical power to attract visitors and hold them spellbound. As innkeeper Helena Harrington says, "The falls call to people."

However, it is rarely, if ever, clear to us what that call implies. The answer is not necessarily apparent even when we are standing at Table Rock, on the deck of the *Maid of the Mist*, or in the Cave of the Winds. We stare at a continuously collapsing wall of water—into the face of the Gorgon, the Giant Horned Serpent, or whatever one wishes to call it—and we do not know what we are seeing. Surely there is something more here than a giant, cascading river. Visitors could be forgiven for throwing their arms in the air and shouting, "What does it all mean?"

Filled to capacity with tourists, a bright red jet boat (opposite) skims over churning waters near the Whirlpool Basin vortex downriver from the falls.

Niagara USA

For much of the nineteenth century, nearly all the land near Niagara Falls was privately owned and subject to the blight of crass commercialism. An unsightly assemblage of mismatched hotels, restaurants, saloons, and oddball tourist attractions lined the Niagara Gorge and the banks of the Niagara River above the falls. Beginning in the late 1860s, however, a "Free Niagara" movement coalesced around landscape architect Frederick Law Olmsted. For nearly twenty years Olmsted pushed for government action in the United States and Canada to acquire critical acreage for a protected park system to be known as the Niagara Reservation. With the help of famed artist Frederic Edwin Church, Olmsted eventually succeeded; in 1885 parks were established in both the United States and Canada to enhance and protect Niagara's scenic wonders.

On the U.S. side of the border is New York's Niagara Falls State Park, which encompasses American Falls, Bridal Veil Falls, and part of Horseshoe Falls. Historically important as the first state park in the United States, it overlooks Niagara Gorge and provides access to the Cave of the Winds, the *Maid of the Mist*, the American Falls Observation Tower, and many other popular attractions. Visitors may enjoy hiking, biking, fishing, nature trails, and an assortment of enticing museums, shops, and restaurants. The park gets millions of visitors each year, most of whom come to enjoy the magnificent views of the waterfalls and gorge. For more information call (716) 278-1796.

Today the park and other Niagara-area destinations are promoted by the Niagara Tourism and Convention Corporation (Niagara USA), formed in 2003. The corporation's stated mission is "to enhance the economic prosperity of Niagara County by promoting, selling, and marketing the County as a premier destination." With Niagara Falls as its centerpiece, the corporation certainly has a lot to offer the traveling public. To contact Niagara USA or plan a Niagara Falls visit, call (800) 338-7890, or visit the NTCC Web site at www.niagara-usa.com.

"People have been trying to read the meaning of Niagara Falls for centuries," says author Elizabeth McKinsey. "Some have looked at this incredibly powerful phenomenon, this vast quantity of water—four great inland seas emptying into Lake Ontario and the St. Lawrence River basin—and have seen it as the power of God channeled between the banks of a river. Many have said the sound of the falls *is* God speaking to them in a voice that is all encompassing and terrifying, yet benevolent, full of promise, and full of hope."

Artists, intellectuals, and others caught up in the romantic movement of the late eighteenth and early nineteenth centuries looked to nature for spiritual inspiration. They studied the natural world for lessons about the deeper meaning of existence. In nature they sensed something higher, nobler, and purer than themselves—something they described as "the sublime."

Europeans found much in the New World that was sublime. There were vast forests and plains, towering mountains and grand plateaus, enormous lakes and endlessly winding rivers. And there was Niagara Falls.

"Niagara Falls is the perfect embodiment of the sublime," says McKinsey. "It's immense, appealing, and awe inspiring, but also terrifying."

North Americans were quick to adopt the concept of the sublime, and not just because European ideas were considered fashionable. They needed a way to relate to nature that didn't necessarily involve taking an ax to a tree, plowing up a virgin prairie, or dynamiting

a mountainside to build a railroad. A sense of the sublime gave them that, and a trip to Niagara Falls provided an opportunity to encounter the sublime in a close and personal way.

"When they looked at Niagara Falls, they not only saw a sublime natural wonder but also the promise of the North American continent," says McKinsey. "North America was supposed to be mostly untouched wilderness, and that's what Niagara Falls represented, even after the land around it became settled and built up."

The vision of Niagara Falls as representative of the sublime would find its way onto the canvases of Frederic Church and other fine artists. It has been captured in pictures from the time of the very earliest daguerreotypes in the 1840s to the present day with our digital photographs and disposable cameras. It has found a voice in poetry and prose. It has even enlivened musical scores.

The notion that a higher, nobler plain can be reached at Niagara Falls has been expressed in other ways as well. Some viewed the feats of tightrope walkers and stunters as sublime. Roebling's 1850s suspension bridge across the Niagara Gorge was seen as sublime. Even the harnessing of the Niagara River with canals, tunnels, and hydroelectric power plants has been described as sublime.

"Yes, the scene we see today is practically nothing like the falls the Native Americans once knew or that the first European explorers witnessed," says McKinsey. "It's paved, and much of the water has been diverted into the power plants. There are restaurants, amenities, restrooms, and railings. But it does still matter that tons of water continue to strike the rocks below the brink every second. That's why Niagara Falls remains North America's best-known natural phenomenon. That's why people still come here, and that's why you find people wandering around Goat Island looking for a secluded place to view and appreciate it. They want to see the water and the rocks. They want to feel the mist. They want to see the rainbow."

Even if half the water is gone, Niagara Falls remains cinema on a really big screen. It's espresso. It gets the blood running. Everyone who sees it for the first time, or the second, or third, or tenth has a word for the scene, and whatever language they are speaking, their word can be translated as "Wow!"

It may have been a musician who put it most eloquently. In 1908 Austrian composer Gustav Mahler, the creator of *Das Lied von der Erde* (*Songs from the Earth*) and many other classics, came to the United States to conduct the New York Philharmonic Orchestra. Mahler took time from his musical duties for a trip to view the natural wonder he had heard so much about throughout his life. Upon seeing the falls, Mahler sucked in his breath and, perhaps picking up a twig and lifting it in the air as if it were a baton, he said:

American Falls at night.

"At last, fortissimo!"

Chronology

18,000 years ago A substantial portion of North America, including the Niagara area, was covered with thick ice sheets. As they advanced southward, the ice sheets gouged out the basins of what would become the Great Lakes.

About 12,500 years ago The Niagara area became free of the ice sheets. Melting ice began to form the lakes and riverbeds.

About 10,500 years ago Glacial meltwaters were rerouted through northern Ontario, bypassing the southern route. For the next 5,000 years, Lake Erie remained only half the size of today, and the quantity of water flowing through the Niagara River and over the falls was significantly less than today.

About 5,500 years ago The meltwaters were once again rerouted through the Niagara region, restoring the river and falls to their full power.

1604 Samuel de Champlain visited the area as early as 1604. Members of his party reported to him about a spectacular waterfall. While he may never have visited Niagara Falls, he wrote about it in his journal.

1650 Niagara Falls was under the control of the Seneca Nation.

1678 Father Louis Hennepin, a Roman Catholic priest, is said by many historians to be the first European to view and describe the falls and bring them to the world's attention. Hennepin was traveling with explorer Rene Robert Cavelier (La Salle).

1687 The French began to settle the area. They built Fort Frontenac at the site of what would later become Fort Niagara. It was called a trading post to appease the Senecas.

1721 French Roman Catholic missionary Father Charlevoix was the first person to give an accurate estimate of the height of the falls. He was also the first person known to have described the shape of the Canadian Falls as a horseshoe.

1726 The French constructed a two-story stone building at what today is Fort Niagara. The structure would become known as the French Castle. Located at the mouth of the Niagara River, this strategic outpost would be held at different times by the French, British, and Americans.

1727 The French smuggled cannons onto the top floor of the French Castle after giving the Indians a generous gift of brandy and intoxicating them. This made the structure a fort.

1759 The first known effort to harness the waters of the falls was made by Daniel Joncairs. He built a small canal above the falls to power his sawmill.

1760 The British arrived in the area and built Fort Schlosser to control the upper end of the Niagara portage road, the most important route for transporting goods and troops to western outposts.

September 14, 1763 A group of young dissident Seneca men ambushed a portage wagon train just above Devil's Hole. They were angry with the British for no longer paying them to help move cargo. The Senecas killed as many as eighty wagon drivers and soldiers, throwing many of their bodies, wagons, and horses into the gorge.

1764 As retribution for attacking British soldiers and settlers the previous year, the Six Nations of the Iroquois Confederation were forced to give the British their lands on both sides of the Niagara River. However, members of the Seneca Nation were permitted to travel through and hunt on the land.

1794 African-American slaves from the United States began using the Niagara River as an escape route to freedom in Canada. (The Canadian Fugitive Slave Act of 1793 allowed slaves to seek asylum in Canada.)

1803 Jerome Bonaparte, younger brother of Napoleon, and his bride visited Niagara Falls. They may have been the first couple to honeymoon at the falls.

1805 Augustus and Peter Porter enlarged the original canal above the falls to provide hydraulic power to their gristmill and tannery.

1812 During the War of 1812, settlements around Niagara Falls were decimated, and Buffalo was burned to the ground.

July 25, 1814 The bloodiest battle of the War of 1812 took place at Lundy's Lane, now the city of Niagara Falls, Ontario.

December 24, 1814 The Treaty of Ghent ended the War of 1812.

1816 There was so much ice accumulation from Lake Erie that by May the American and Bridal Veil Falls had slowed to just a trickle.

May 1816 The devotion of a father resulted in the renaming of the islands above Niagara Falls. Parkhurst Whitney enjoyed taking his three young daughters and infant son to visit the islands. They especially liked exploring four beautiful little islands south of Goat Island. Whitney approached the owners of the islands about naming the tiny islands after his children. Since then, they have been known as the Three Sisters Islands and Little Brother Island.

1819 The Boundary Commissioners for Canada and the United States confirmed the original International Boundary Line for the two nations along the Niagara River established by Jay's Treaty of 1794.

October 26, 1825 The Erie Canal opened, linking the waters of Lake Erie in the west to the Hudson River in the east. It was the engineering marvel of its day. Today it is mostly used by recreational boats rather than giant cargo-carrying barges.

1825 The Cataract House opened. It would become one of Niagara's best-known and longest operating hotels. Among its famous guests were Abraham Lincoln, Grover Cleveland, Winston Churchill, and Franklin Roosevelt. The hotel was destroyed by fire in 1945.

October 17, 1829 What is believed to have been the first of many Niagara Falls stunts occurred when Sam Patch, a twenty-two-year-old from Rhode Island, jumped off a platform at the top of a 98-foot-high ladder set up near Goat Island. A huge crowd watched as Patch jumped into the turbulent water, popped to the surface, and swam to shore.

November 27, 1829 The first Welland Canal opened, allowing vessels traveling from Lake Ontario to the upper Niagara River to avoid the falls and rapids and negating the need for a portage.

1833 Construction of the stone, circular Terrapin Tower provided visitors with incredible views of Horseshoe Falls. It was torn down in 1873.

1836 The first railroad started service between Niagara Falls and Buffalo, using horse-drawn cars.

1846 The first *Maid of the Mist* was launched to transport people, luggage, mail, and cargo across the Niagara River below the falls. It did well until 1848, when a suspension bridge across the gorge dramatically curtailed business.

1848 Increased tourism led to a demand for passage over the Niagara River and the building of the Charles Ellet's Niagara Suspension Bridge. It was supplanted in 1855 by John Roebling's Niagara Falls Suspension Bridge.

1848 The *Maid of the Mist* was recast as a sightseeing venture.

March 29–30, 1848 A massive ice dam formed on the Niagara River near Buffalo, preventing water from reaching the falls. Around midnight, the American and Bridal Veil Falls stopped completely, while Horseshoe Falls was reduced to a small waterfall at its center. The next day an amazed local populace explored the nearly dry riverbed. That evening the ice dam broke, restoring the normal flow of the river and falls.

1857 Frederic Edwin Church, a New York artist, sat at Table Rock on the Canadian side and made the sketches he would use to create *Niagara,* the most famous painting of Horseshoe Falls.

June 30, 1859 Niagara Falls's first and greatest tightrope walker, Jean Francois Gravelet, alias the Great Blondin, made his first walk across the gorge. A thirty-five-year-old Frenchman, he made twenty-one crossings on a 1,100-foot rope stretched from Prospect Park to the Canadian side. For one of his most famous stunts, Blondin carried his agent across the gorge on his back.

August 15, 1860 As tricks on the tightrope escalated, anything seemed possible. William Hunt, alias Farini the Great, of Port Hope, Ontario, carried a washing machine on his back to the center of the rope across the gorge. He lowered a pail to the river, drew up water, and washed a handkerchief.

September 14, 1860 Horseshoe Falls was artificially illuminated for the first time. About 200 white and colored flares of the type used at sea to signal for help were placed at three locations. The spectacular illumination was a celebration for the visit by the Prince of Wales, later King Edward the VII, as part of his tour of Canada.

June 15, 1861 Joel Robinson and two crewmen piloted the recently sold *Maid of the Mist* boat through the lower rapids to Queenston, Ontario. The trip was through 3 miles of wild water and took just seventeen minutes but made a lasting impression.

January 1, 1869 The Upper Suspension Bridge opened about one-eighth of a mile below the American Falls. With a span of 1,268 feet, it was one of the longest suspension bridges in the world at the time. Not long after it opened, an elevator was installed inside the Canadian tower, providing visitors willing to pay ten cents with a new view of the falls.

August 25, 1873 Henry Bellini (the "Australian Blondin") started his semiweekly treks on a 1,500-foot-long rope across the gorge. It was the longest rope ever used at Niagara Falls.

July 1876 The only female tightrope walker to perform at Niagara Falls was twenty-three-year-old Maria Spelterini. A former circus performer, she matched nearly all the stunts performed by her male counterparts. Her tricks included walking across a rope with her feet fastened inside peach baskets, waltzing across the rope, and crossing while blindfolded.

January 1879 Electricity was used for the first time to illuminate the falls. The lights used had an illumination power of 32,000 candles, a fraction of the intensity of the lights used today.

1881 Commercial hydroelectric power was produced for the first time using direct current to illuminate the nearby village of Niagara Falls. The Niagara Falls Hydraulic Power & Manufacturing Company built its Power Station No. 1 at the top of the gorge, just below the American Falls.

1883 The Niagara Falls Power Company hired George Westinghouse to design a system to generate alternating current.

July 24, 1883 Captain Matthew Webb, believed to have been the first person to swim across the English Channel, failed in his attempt to swim through the Whirlpool Rapids. Webb was hit by a large wave and disappeared under the water. His body was found four days later.

1885 This was a pivotal year in the history of Niagara Falls, as both American and Canadian officials began to preserve land for future public use. The Free Niagara movement in the United States, led by Frederick Law Olmsted and artist Frederic Church, encouraged the State of New York to buy land to become part of the Niagara Reservation State Park. Later the Niagara Parks Commission was established in Canada with the mandate "to preserve and enhance the natural beauty of the falls and the Niagara River corridor for the enjoyment of visitors, while maintaining our financial independence."

A BEAUTIFUL ENGINEERING STRUCTURE
NIAGARA FALLS (NEW) SUSPENSION BRIDGE

Spans the wonderful gorge of the NIAGARA, giving the visitor and tourist a GRAND VIEW of the AMERICAN and HORSESHOE FALLS, as well as of the river up and down the gorge. Bridge toll over and back, 15 cents.

July 15, 1885 The first state park in the United States opened. Niagara Reservation State Park was designed by Frederick Law Olmsted, the landscape architect who designed Central Park in New York City and Delaware Park in Buffalo. The park provides panoramic views of the falls.

1886 The wood-and-stone bridge over the Niagara River was replaced by a predominantly steel structure that continues to carry trains across the river.

July 11, 1886 The first barrel stunt at Niagara Falls was attempted by Carlisle D. Graham, from Philadelphia, who rode an oak barrel through the Whirlpool Rapids.

August 22, 1886 William J. Kendall swam through the Whirlpool Rapids. The Boston policeman wore a cork life preserver and suffered only minor injuries.

November 28, 1886 George Hazlett took his girlfriend, Sadie Allen, on an unusual date—a ride through the Whirlpool Rapids in a barrel. They both survived.

New Rainbow Bridge, Niagara Falls, N. Y.

December 11, 1886 Alphonse "Professor" King took an unusual "walk" across the river below the falls. The thirty-one-year-old Frenchman bet some men that he could "walk" a hundred feet on the water. He used a set of shoes made of tin that were 32 inches long, 8 inches wide, and 9 inches deep. He made two attempts. Both times he fell into the river and had to be rescued.

June 22, 1887 Stephen Peer, known by the stage name "Professor Peere," walked on the thinnest cable ever stretched across the gorge. It wasn't to be his most memorable Niagara Falls stunt, however (see below).

June 25, 1887 Peer became the only person to fall to his death while walking on a tightrope across the gorge. The circumstances of his death remain clouded in mystery. One story suggests that Peer and two companions were on the platform where he typically started his performance. Peer began his walk on the cable but fell, without a sound, 45 feet to his death. There was speculation that the men had been drinking.

August 16, 1887 Alphonse "Professor" King returned to the falls to attempt a stunt almost as unusual as his attempt to "walk" on water a year earlier. He pedaled a "Water Bicycle" around the lower river, making one trip across the river in less than five minutes.

May 24, 1888 Queen Victoria Park in Ontario opened on Victoria Day. Its 154 acres are the heart of the Niagara Parks system. It features well-manicured gardens, spectacular views of the falls, and underground observation rooms that provide the illusion of being within the falling waters.

June 8, 1888 Almost two years earlier George Hazlett and William Potts had used a barrel to ride through the Whirlpool Rapids. Now, as a precursor to their own planned attempt to go over Horseshoe Falls, they sent a white bantam rooster over the falls in the barrel. When the rooster failed to survive, the two men wisely changed their minds.

1895 The Niagara Falls Power Company began operating the world's first alternating-current central power station about 7,000 feet above the American Falls.

July 15, 1895 The Great Gorge Route electric railway started operating. Trolley cars took passengers from Niagara Falls, New York, into the gorge and to the village of Lewiston. At the time, many questioned the wisdom of building a trolley line in such a dangerous location.

July 1, 1896 James E. Hardy became the youngest person to cross the gorge on a tightrope.

1897 The first steel archway bridge near the falls was completed to carry vehicles and pedestrians between Canada and the United States. It is known today as the Whirlpool Rapids Bridge.

1900 Henry Perky, inventor of Shredded Wheat, the Triscuit cracker, and the machinery used to manufacture them, brought the Natural Food Company to Niagara Falls.

July 9, 1900 Peter Nissen, alias P. M. Bowser, from Chicago, made his first attempt to negotiate the Whirlpool Rapids in a boat. After helplessly circling the whirlpool four times in his boat, *Fool Killer,* he was rescued and towed to shore. He was badly shaken by the experience and said he would never try such a stunt again. He would change his mind, however (see below).

1901 Theodore Roosevelt, later the twenty-sixth president of the United States, visited Niagara Falls.

1901 During the Pan-American Exposition in Buffalo, searchlights illuminated the American and Horseshoe Falls.

1901 The Shredded Wheat Plant in Niagara Falls was called the "Palace of Light" because it had 844 windows comprising 30,000 panes of glass. It embodied Henry Perky's vision of an ideal factory.

August 6, 1901 Joe Chamber was the first man to successfully swim through the Whirlpool Rapids.

September 6, 1901 President McKinley visited Niagara Falls, including a trip to Goat Island, lunch at the International Hotel, and a tour of the Niagara Falls Power Company's power station.

September 6, 1901 Martha E. Wagenfuhrer made a successful trip through Whirlpool Rapids in a barrel.

September 7, 1901 Using the same barrel as Martha Wagenfuhrer from the previous day, Maude Willard rode a barrel through the Whirlpool Rapids with her pet fox terrier. As the barrel drifted in the dangerous waters for hours, the dog's nose became stuck in the barrel's only air hole, suffocating Willard.

October 12, 1901 Peter Nissen decided to repeat his trip through the Whirlpool Rapids in a boat. This time he used a larger steam-powered vessel called *Fool Killer No. 2.* The boat was badly damaged but Nissen again survived.

October 24, 1901 Annie Edson Taylor is the first person to go over the falls in a barrel and survive. The widowed schoolteacher from Bay City, Michigan, took her trip over the Horseshoe Falls in an oak barrel. Taylor performed this reckless stunt in order to make money to pay her debts and avoid ending up in the poorhouse in her old age. While her stunt was successful, she didn't achieve her goal (see below).

September 6, 1904 The archbishop of Canterbury visited Niagara Falls, touring the Niagara Falls Power Company and riding the Great Gorge Route train.

1905 The Niagara Movement, a civil rights organization, first met in Buffalo and Canada. This meeting is identified as the precursor to the formation of the NAACP a few years later.

1906 The Government of Ontario brought power transmission operations under public control, distributing Niagara's power to many parts of the province.

Summer 1910 Oscar Williams made several crossings of the gorge on a wire. However, public interest in tightrope walking had waned, and his stunts drew small crowds.

June 27, 1911 A California pilot successfully completed one of the most unusual stunts ever tried at the falls. Lincoln J. Beachy took off in a biplane from a field in Niagara Falls, New York, and flew right over the brink of the Horseshoe Falls. As about 20,000 people watched, he descended deep into the gorge and flew under the arches of the Falls View Bridge. "It was a flight filled with more dangers than you can imagine," Beachy later said.

July 25, 1911 Niagara Falls native Bobby Leach was the first man to survive going over Horseshoe Falls in a barrel. Leach used a steel barrel. He was badly bruised and bleeding when rescuers pulled him from the barrel.

February 4, 1912 On a bitterly cold day, one of the grand traditions of the falls tragically ended when the ice bridge below the falls broke up without warning. Most of the people on the bridge at the time were able to swim ashore, but an ice floe with three men on it floated downriver toward the Whirlpool Rapids. Attempts to rescue the men with ropes thrown from the two bridges over the rapids failed. The three were tossed into the water and never seen again. Afterward, people were no longer permitted to go onto the ice bridges, ending an era at the falls.

August 8, 1916 The Niagara Aero Car Company started carrying passengers on a ten-minute, 1,770-foot trip just 250 feet above the Whirlpool Rapids.

August 6, 1918 A scow being towed up the Niagara River broke free from a tug and got caught in the river's dangerous currents. Two crewmen aboard the steel barge were able to ground the craft in a shallow section of the Canadian Rapids, only 2,500 feet from the brink of Horseshoe Falls. Much of the day was spent trying to rescue the men. The next morning the exhausted crewmen were finally brought ashore. Left behind in the rapids, the scow has slowly rusted away, but parts of it remain as a visible proof of the dangers of the falls.

July 11, 1920 Charles Stephens, fifty-eight, a barber from Bristol, England, went over the Horseshoe Falls in an oak barrel weighing 600 pounds. Stephens hoped to make enough money from the stunt to be able to stop cutting hair. He stopped, but not for the reason he had hoped. "But suppose you don't come back," he was asked by a reporter. "No use supposin'," Stephens said, "you does it or you doesn't. I bet I does." Stephens was killed when he took the plunge.

September 6, 1920 A rock fell from the ceiling at the Cave of the Winds, killing three people and injuring several others.

April 29, 1921 Annie Taylor's efforts to make money from her stunt never materialized. The first person to survive going over the falls in a barrel ended up in the Niagara County Infirmary, where she died a poor woman. A collection was taken to give her a proper burial at the Oakwood Cemetery in Niagara Falls, New York.

1925 Elevators were installed at Cave of the Winds to quickly transport tourists to the bottom of the cave, turning this popular destination into a major tourist attraction.

1925 The Niagara Falls Illumination Board was created to finance, operate, and maintain a permanent illumination system. The falls have been illuminated most nights since that time. Current board members include the City of Niagara Falls, New York; the City of Niagara Falls, Ontario; New York State Office of Parks, Recreation and Historic Preservation; Ontario Power Generation; and the Niagara Parks Commission.

July 4, 1928 French-Canadian Joseph Albert "Jean" Lussier went over Horseshoe Falls on the U.S. Independence Day in a 1,037-pound rubber ball built around two steel-frame pieces. Lussier not only survived but also took his ball on tour and showed movies of his experience.

July 5, 1930 George L. Stathakis survived his plunge over Horseshoe Falls, only to die when his barrel was trapped for sixteen hours by the force of the falling water. A Buffalo author and philosopher, Stathakis planned to profit from his exploit by selling the motion picture rights for his trip. Stathakis took along his hundred-year-old pet turtle, "Sonny Boy." The turtle survived but was unable to keep Stathakis's promise to reporters that if he didn't make it the turtle would someday reveal the secret of the trip.

September 17, 1935 A landslide buried a large section of track on the Great Gorge Route railway. The largest and most expensive of many such incidents, the rockfall resulted in the closing of the railway. During its forty years in operation, the rail line carried thirteen million tourists.

January 27, 1938 The Honeymoon Bridge collapsed into the river due to pressure from a 60-foot ice jam. Because of the impending danger, engineers had closed the heavily traveled bridge the day before.

June 7, 1939 King George VI and Queen Elizabeth, parents of Queen Elizabeth II, visited Niagara Falls.

November 1, 1941 The Rainbow Bridge was formally opened. It was built at a cost of $3.7 million by the Niagara Falls Bridge Commission, an agency formed by the New York State Legislature and the Province of Ontario. At the time it was built, its 950-foot steel arch was the longest hingeless arch in the world.

1949 Jawaharlal Nehru, prime minister of India, visited Niagara Falls.

August 5, 1951 The death of a famous local riverman and daredevil prompted both Canadian and American authorities to try to better regulate stunts at the falls. However, their efforts were no more successful than the man who lost his life. William "Red" Hill Jr., thirty-eight, went over Horseshoe Falls in a frail-looking device he called "The Thing." About 200,000 spectators watched as pieces of the contraption popped to the surface below the falls. Hill's battered body was recovered the next morning.

1952 Marilyn Monroe and Joseph Cotten filmed the movie *Niagara*, shot entirely on the Canadian side of Niagara Falls.

July 28, 1954 The largest rockfall ever recorded at Niagara Falls occurred near Prospect Point. The section that fell was 360 feet long, 130 feet wide, and weighed about 185,000 tons. The incident made a significant addition to the area below the American and Bridal Veil Falls, where rocks have been accumulating for hundreds of years.

1955 The original Cave of the Winds was destroyed by a controlled dynamite blast. The cave had become too dangerous for tourists.

April 22, 1955 The two *Maid of the Mists* boats were destroyed by fire before the tourist season even started. A 40-foot open yacht was quickly launched as *The Little Maid*, saving the tourist season.

June 7, 1956 Nearly two-thirds of Schoellkopf Power Station was destroyed by hundreds of tons of rock, concrete, and rubble. Damages were estimated at $100 million.

July 9, 1960 The date of "the Miracle at Niagara Falls." James Honeycutt took two of his friend's children for a ride in his 14-foot aluminum boat. Deanne Woodward, seventeen, and her seven-year-old brother Roger got the ride of a lifetime. The trip began several miles above the falls, but Honeycutt decided to take the children close to the Canadian Rapids. He got too close and was drawn into the rampaging current. The boat overturned, tossing all three into the rapids. Deanne struggled to get close to shore, where she was rescued by several brave tourists only 15 feet from the edge of the falls. Roger and Jim were swept over the falls. The captain of the *Maid of the Mist*, Clifford Keech, spotted Roger in the water just below the falls and pulled him onto the deck. Roger suffered only minor injuries. Honeycutt was not as fortunate; his body was recovered four days later.

1961 The huge state-owned Robert Moses Power Plant opened.

July 15, 1961 William Fitzgerald became the first African American to go over the waterfalls in a barrel. Fitzgerald, alias Nathan Boya, went over Horseshow Falls in a ball he named "The Plunge-o-sphere," a steel frame covered with rubber. He suffered only minor scrapes and bruises—and paid a fine of $113.

1967 Alexei N. Kosygin, Soviet premier, visited Niagara Falls.

June 12 to November 26, 1969 Man brings the thundering falls to a halt. Water flow to the American Falls was almost completely cut off by the U.S. Army Corps of Engineers to study erosion and rock formations.

August 5, 1969 The first fatal sightseeing helicopter accident near the falls took place. Mechanical failure caused an American copter to crash into the Canadian Rapids, killing the pilot and two passengers.

June 11, 1977 Karel Soucek, a thirty-year-old native of Hamilton, Ontario, started his daredevil career when he rode a 300-pound discarded oil tank through Whirlpool Rapids. Canadian officials needed a helicopter to rescue him, but it was only the beginning for Soucek (see below).

1979 Superman rescued Lois Lane from the Whirlpool Rapids in scenes from the popular *Superman II* movie.

1983 Soviet official Mikhail Gorbachev, later president of the U.S.S.R., and Soviet ambassador to Canada Alexander Yakovlev visited Niagara Falls.

1983 Canadian prime minister Pierre Trudeau visited Niagara Falls.

July 3, 1984 Karel Soucek used his success riding the Whirlpool Rapids seven years earlier to attempt to go over the falls. He went over Horseshoe Falls in a bright-red plastic barrel. Printed on the outside of the barrel was the slogan LAST OF NIAGARA'S DAREDEVILS. As with many who preceded him, Soucek believed he could reap great financial rewards from his feat. He planned to re-create his stunt in public arenas. His first attempt, at the Houston Astrodome, ended with his death when his wooden barrel fell 180 feet.

1985 Li Xiannian, president of the People's Republic of China, visited Niagara Falls.

July 28, 1985 Dave Munday failed in his first attempt to go over Horseshoe Falls in a barrel. He was arrested, fined, and put on two-year probation. But he didn't give up (see below).

August 18, 1985 Steven Trotter, who wanted to become a professional stunt-man, went over Horseshoe Falls in a modified pickle barrel lined on the inside with foam packing. Trotter described the trip "like an elevator with no cables." His stunt provided some short-lived fame, including an appearance on the *Tonight Show* with Johnny Carson, but he never became a professional stuntman. Trotter's barrel is on display at the Daredevil Museum in Niagara Falls, New York.

October 5, 1985 Ignoring warnings from authorities, Dave Munday made a successful trip over Horseshoe Falls. His red-and-white barrel contained a two-way radio, an oxygen tank, and a mounted video camera. Munday escaped going to jail, but he was fined $1,500—not enough to discourage his fascination with the falls (see below).

1987 The Duke and Duchess of York, Prince Andrew and Sarah Ferguson, visited Niagara Falls.

September 27, 1989 Peter DeBernardi and Jeffrey J. Petkovich became the first twosome to go over Horseshoe Falls and survive. The two Canadians converted a 12-foot-long, 3,000-pound tank for their late-afternoon ride. The tank contained two compartments with hammocks, seatbelts, Plexiglas windows, and a video camera to document the trip. Neither man was injured.

March 30, 1990 Magician David Copperfield appeared on a CBS television special called "The Niagara Challenge."

June 5, 1990 Jessie Sharp, a twenty-eight-year-old from Tennessee, died after his early-afternoon trip over Horseshoe Falls. As Sharp floated down the Canadian Rapids in his polyethylene kayak, officials at Ontario Hydro tried to lower the water by using control gates located just above the rapids. Sharp maneuvered around shallow spots and large boulders, determined to reach the falls. The slightly damaged kayak was recovered, but Sharp's body was never found.

1991 Princess Diana of Wales and her sons, Prince William and Prince Harry, visited Niagara Falls and took a ride on the *Maid of the Mist*.

September 29, 1992 Two sightseeing helicopters, one from the United States and the other from Canada, collided near Horseshoe Falls. The American copter crashed at the foot of the Niagara Parks Incline Railway, killing the pilot and three passengers. The Canadian copter landed safely in the parking lot at Marineland. The pilot suffered minor injuries; his four passengers were unhurt.

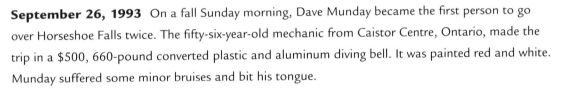

September 26, 1993 On a fall Sunday morning, Dave Munday became the first person to go over Horseshoe Falls twice. The fifty-six-year-old mechanic from Caistor Centre, Ontario, made the trip in a $500, 660-pound converted plastic and aluminum diving bell. It was painted red and white. Munday suffered some minor bruises and bit his tongue.

June 18, 1995 Around nine o'clock on a Sunday morning, Steve Trotter and Lori Martin became the first male/female duo to successfully ride a barrel over Horseshoe Falls. They were rescued from the rocks just below the falls by Canadian authorities. Trotter, thirty-two, and Martin, twenty-nine, were arrested and fined. Neither was seriously injured. Trotter is the same man who went over the falls alone in 1985.

1996 Former U.S. president Jimmy Carter and his wife, Rosalynn, visited Niagara Falls.

1996 One of North America's most venerable tourist attractions, the *Maid of the Mist*, celebrated its 150th anniversary. The postal services of the United States and Canada participated in a joint commemorative stamp cancellation event.

December 9, 1996 Casino Niagara opened in Niagara Falls, Ontario.

1997–98 New fixtures replaced outdated lamps and fixtures, doubling the intensity of the lights on the falls. Twenty-one xenon lights are used to illuminate the falls in a rainbow of colors.

2002 The Seneca Niagara Casino opened in Niagara Falls, New York.

Thousands of years from now More than 90 percent of the water from the upper Niagara River flows into the Canadian Rapids and over Horseshoe Falls. That means the waterfall will continue to recede and create a beautiful gorge. Much less water flows over the American and Bridal Veil Falls, so it is likely that over time they will become a steep rapid until Horseshoe Falls passes Goat Island. Then the upper river will direct all of its water to Horseshoe Falls, drying up the American and Bridal Veil Falls. But that won't happen for thousands of years.

Index

Page numbers in **bold** refer to illustrations.